"Putting Up With Leona"

Survival in the kitchen

By: Leona J. Wells

My profound gratitude to
Angie Miller
and
Heather L. Randell

Without their talents and wisdom, this
endeavor would not have become a reality

Photos by
Angie Miller Photo Art

Contents

Discover the Spirit

In October of 1989, as our family crossed the Canadian Border on our journey from Alaska to North Dakota, a feeling came over me that I never would have associated with being in North Dakota. It was strange, I hadn't lived in North Dakota for 35 years, and yet I felt I was coming home.

The North Dakota license plate says, "Discover the Spirit." I was feeling it — the deeper we traveled into North Dakota the more consumed I was by its peace.

Again and again I have discovered that spirit. It came early one morning as I stood on the front porch at the historical Bagg Farm near Mooreton, where our church group was participating in a service project. Other volunteers were elsewhere, and I was alone in the quiet of that beautiful summer morning.

My mind traveled back in time and I could imagine myself 100 years earlier, greeting the same sun and feeling the soft breeze on my face. It seemed I was not alone. There was the presence of another woman, from another time, sweeping the porch, preparing for the coming day. For a moment, I was privileged to feel the pioneer spirit.

I've stood in a wheat field at harvest time as a hot summer breeze turns the entire field into rolling waves. The crickets call out their approval and seemed to echo what I was feeling. "Discover the Spirit."

It was the spirit of the earth. The rolling thunder of an approaching prairie storm, the sun setting over a corn field, the cooing dove that faithfully wakes me each spring and summer morning.

That spirit has enveloped me as I stood at my grandfather and grandmother's graves, as I placed a flower near the headstone. I studied the stone that bears the inscription of Ole Graff: born 12 June 1887, Died 8 June 1982. Then there's Emma Haugen Graff: born 28 April 1890, died 22 May 1989.

The stone speaks an untruth to me. It gives dates that try to convince me that my grandparents are gone. Were they like the flower placed beside the stone that would wither away? Is it true what people say, "Nothing lasts forever?"

I lift my eyes and gaze over the countryside to a road that is still gravel.

In my mind's eye I watch as a black 46 Chevy Coupe heads north. I see myself in the back seat. Grandpa is driving. He isn't saying anything. He never said much to me, or to children in general. Children were to be seen, and not heard.

Maybe another reason I was riding in the back was because he kept his spittoon (a coffee can) on the floor of the passenger side. Even at my young age, I knew he wouldn't hit the can every time.

As I leaned over the front seat with my chin on my hands, I could see the hard road fast approaching. I may have been born at night, but it wasn't last night, so I knew enough about cars to know it was time to start slowing down. Grandpa wasn't slowing down.

I was also smart enough to know you don't counsel Grandpa. So I said nothing. With eyes as big as saucers, I looked both ways to see if any cars were coming as we flew over the hard road and continued onto the gravel.

Before I knew what I was doing, I heard myself correcting Grandpa. "Grandpa, you went through that stop sign." Without turning around he dryly stated, "Ya, vell, I've been here a lot longer den dat sign." I got off easy; nothing else was said.

Ole was set in his ways. That was no secret. Some things were written in granite. Like his Norwegian heritage, or the fact that Lutherans marry Lutherans and America's salvation was in the Republican Party. Once in a while someone forgot about Ole's ways.

Mr. Nick Schmidt, a neighbor, was just trying to do the neighborly thing by giving Ole a sack of apples. Who would hold that against a neighbor? But, Mr. Schmidt overlooked one small detail. On the sack in which he placed the apples was an advertisement for Quentin Burdick, who was running for Lt. Governor—a Democrat - Grandpa wouldn't take the apples.

Added to Grandpa's list of constants would be coffee and snooze.

Grandma used to say, "Ole you're not going to live very long if you don't quit chewing dat snooze." He left us at 95.

The hot prairie wind rustling the trees brings me back to the present. I gaze down at the granite stone again. Emma's name forces my eyes to look over to the direction where the farmhouse once stood. My eyes refuse to accept the fact that the house is gone along with the enormous barn, the chicken coop, and my favorite chestnut crabapple tree. Yet in my mind I see everything as it stood so long ago, even the hollyhocks around the outhouse.

I see myself again. This time I'm picking potato bugs off the potato plants in Grandma's garden. "One cent a bug," she said she would pay me. I know I picked one million bugs off those plants, but my wage was always one dollar. Long into my adulthood, I would receive $1 in every birthday card from Grandma.

Inside the farmhouse was a room that will be etched in my mind forever: 'The Parlor." Children were not allowed beyond those closed doors. So naturally I made it my goal to explore that forbidden realm.

I remember the day I quietly crept through those hallowed doors, while Grandma was cleaning the separator out in the barn. Slowly I pushed open the door, and was immediately in awe as my eyes drank in the perfectness of that celestial room.

Its orderliness demanded reverence. Reverent I was as I sat down on the red velvet couch with its white doilies draped over its arms and back. Directly in front of me a potted green vine created its own jungle, as it wrapped around and around its container on the coffee table. African violets were blooming on the table by the window.

Outside, the day had been hot and the humidity was high, but the parlor was cool, an oasis. How long I sat there, I don't know. But knowing I shouldn't push my luck, I left as quietly as I came. The parlor experience has never left me.

Often I think of the changes my grandparents experienced. Their lives began with horse and buggies. They saw wonderful changes come into their world—the car, electricity, telephone, radio, television, jets and men on the moon.

Grandpa was of the opinion we messed up on a lot of things. One evening he offered his opinion on the state of the moon. "It just doesn't look da same yah know, since dey landed on it."

To me, Grandma had poise and grace. I never saw her wear slacks, although some say she did toward the end of her life. I couldn't imagine Grandma wearing slacks to church, any more than I could imagine Grandpa working in the field on the Sabbath. It just didn't seem right to them.

I don't think there is anyone who can think of Grandma without thinking of food.

At least six different kinds of cookies and bars, flat bread, or lefse would be placed on the table if one dropped by for coffee. My mouth still waters when I think of her pickled crabapples and beets. The root cellar was always full of home canning. If you were stranded for three months in the winter, you could live off what Grandma had stored up.

People are wrong. Some things do last forever. My memories of Ole and Emma, few though they may be, will go with me into eternity. Are Grandpa and Grandma really gone? That 'coming home' feeling tells me, 'no!' If they are gone, why do I still see them every time we drive by where the farm used to be? What about Grandma's influence on my life? She lives on in me.

Come visit and you'll see. I don't drink coffee, but I have pickled beets and apples in the basement and I could feed you for three months from the cellar.

We'll sit down and have a good conversation about how my Grandpa was right. The moon really doesn't look the same since they landed on it. '"Discover the Spirit," it lives on in me.

It lives on in the old pioneer adage, "FIX IT UP, WEAR IT OUT, MAKE IT DO, OR DO WITHOUT."

And so now it's time for me to take up the gauntlet and pass that spirit unto my grandchildren.

In 123 pages I have emptied my brain of principles I have gleaned through the years on how to survive the vicissitudes of life. And most of it centers on food.

Kind of pathetic if you think about it! All one knows on 123 pages. So be it.

Regardless, I am passionate about this.

<u>If you cannot function (survive) in the kitchen, you will never get ahead in life.</u>

You will notice there is no exclamation or comma at the end of the previous sentence. Period – end of discussion.

So let's go into the kitchen because it's time to…. "Put Up With Leona."

Lesson One ~ Gleaning

First of all let me be perfectly clear...gleaning is not begging!!

Webster's Unabridged Dictionary defines gleaning as "to gather laboriously, grain or anything of the like after the regular reapers have harvested." Notice the word laboriously. That means hard work.

It was in October, many years ago, when we moved to our small town in North Dakota. We felt pretty vulnerable, because we were used to canning in preparation for the upcoming winter. It had been an extremely rough year for us financially, so we knew every dime would have to be watched carefully.

My husband has always said I could stretch a dollar from here to New York. (That was when we lived in Seattle)

As we walked around our new little community, we began to notice there were quite a few apple trees that had not been picked. There had not been a hard freeze as yet, and the apples were all in perfect condition.

We decided to knock on a few doors to see if the apples were going to be used. One elderly gentleman told us to pick everything we wanted off the three trees in his yard.

The local bar had plenty of boxes with handles that were just the right size for gathering the apples in.

We put a poster up at the post office and asked if anyone had jars they were no longer using, and said we would be more than happy to pick them up. We were surprised at the number of senior citizens who no longer were canning, and just wanted to get rid of the jars from their basements. We ended up with around 20 cases of free jars.

That fall we canned applesauce, apple pie filling, jelly and apple juice. Our stash lasted until the next apple season. Our expenditure on the venture was the cost of sugar and lids for the jars.

I have since had many opportunities to glean food that would otherwise go to waste.

In September, a common phrase we hear from all our neighbors is "I am so sick of tomatoes. Do you want what's left in my garden?"

Most people do not like waste, and are more than happy to know that what is left in their gardens could be used by someone. That someone should be you. All you have to do is ask.

There are certain rules we have learned to follow when gleaning from others.

First: Always leave the area you picked cleaner than you found it. Pull the tomato vines and haul them off if you have the means. Rake under the apple tree and throw away the rotten apples. Be very careful of tree limbs and vines.

Second: Remember the elderly gentleman that shared his apples with us? Well, after we finished putting up all the apples he let us glean, we visited him with a basket of treasures. He looked at us with an amazed expression on his face as he lifted out the apple jelly, applesauce and the warm apple crisp. As he sat down at his kitchen table, shaking his head in disbelief he said, "For years I have been letting people pick my apples. This is the first time anyone has ever brought me anything in return."

It's so important to give back. I've only had it backfire on me once.

There was an apricot tree down the street that was left unpicked, and apricots were falling on the ground. We asked for permission to pick them, and the owner was more than happy to have the "messy" tree taken care of.

As soon as we were finished making the most marvelous apricot jam we had ever tasted, we took several jars over and thanked them for the apricots.

About a week later I received a call from the tree owner. "Did you really make this jam from the apricots on my tree? I assured her that we had. "Wow, this is the best jam I have ever tasted," she said.

That was the last year she ever offered her apricots to anyone. Dang!! At the time it was the only apricot tree in town.

Gleaning can also apply to commercial farming. Every year during the potato and onion harvest, we glean enough of each to last us well beyond the winter months.

Once again, you only need to ask. We have found that most farmers are happy to let you go in, after their harvesters are done and glean through what is left.

Gleaning in commercial areas has a few additional rules after you've gained permission.

First: Stay out of their way. Pick on the opposite side where the harvesters are working.

Second: Do not pick where harvesting has not taken place.

Third: Always gather enough extra to share with the elderly, or anyone else that does not have the ability to gather themselves. I have to admit this rule has selfish undertones for me. Whenever we have shared with the widows in town, we always end up with cookies or some type of fresh baked bread on our doorstep.

Remember the widow Ruth, the great-grandmother of King David, gleaned in the fields of Boaz, and because of her hard work; both she and Naomi's lives were saved.

Gleaning is a symbiotic endeavor. No farmer or gardener likes to see waste when it comes to his or her labors. Then there are many who for one reason or another do not have gardens. Working together, waste can be done away with and grocery bills can be cut in half.

Happy Gleaning!

The Apple Press

An apple press can be costly but it doesn't take too long before you get your money's worth. I consider it one of my most important kitchen survival tools. We not only make our juice for the year, but use what we don't put up for ourselves, to trade with others for food I may not have grown.

Along with pumpkins and horseradish, it is one of the last projects we do in the "putting up" season. We gather apples from as many different types of apple trees as we can, so every batch tastes a little different. We will press about fifteen bushels in one event.

This is a time when we get all the family and friends together that we can. It's a lot a work so the more hands the better. First, we dump several bushels of apples in a huge tub filled with water. All this does, is get any dust that may have accumulated, while they were sitting in the garage.

As many people as can fit around the tub of apples, they will cut the larger apples in half, and cut off any rotten spots. We then fill up the buckets that will be used, to dump the cut-up apples into the press. With our press a five-gallon bucket of cut up apples is about all the press can hold at one time.

Everyone gets a turn at turning the crank. Children love this part. Especially the young boys who like to show their strength.

The juice is pressed and we fill up quart jars that go immediately into the freezer.

Everyone gets to drink his or her fill of fresh pressed apple juice in addition to filling a gallon to take home.

It never gets old watching the expression on everyone's face as they experience fresh apple juice.

My favorite moments are in January and February when we pull out a quart of apple juice from the freezer for breakfast.

That same expression is once again on our faces as I hear my husband repeat his favorite mealtime statement; "You can't get this in the grocery store!"

Apple Crisp

I use our ground-fall apples or the apples that start to go soft, around January for making apple crisp. You may even have apples on your counter that start to show their age. Don't waste them. Cut off the bad spots and use them in crisp.

So peel your apples and cut into small wedges, enough to fill up a generously buttered pie pan.

Sprinkle ¾ cup of white or brown sugar and around 1½ Tablespoons of cinnamon over the apples.

In a separate bowl mix, 1½ cup of flour (half of the flour can be whole wheat if you wish) ½ cup of brown sugar, 1 cup of butter (chopped into pea size bits), 1 cup of oatmeal, 1 cup of chopped walnuts (optional). Mix thoroughly with your hands and sprinkle over the apple mixture.

Bake at 375° for around 45 minutes. It could be less time or more, depending on the apples and your oven. The apples should be tender and the mixture on top should be golden brown when done. We serve it hot, with homemade whipped cream or vanilla ice cream. Once again, "You can't buy that in the store."

Lesson Two ~ Divide & Multiply

Right out of the gate you need to understand that these lessons are not about nutrition, and I am also not about wowing you with all those gourmet recipes, that are displayed in the grocery store magazines.

So what am I up to, you may ask.

What I am about to share with you is about survival, pure and simple.

You will want to follow what I have to say, if you are sometimes having too much month at the end of the money, or if there are times when your children go to school with an empty tummy, or go to bed at night after a less than filling supper. (You'll have to get used to that little supper anomaly. In the Midwest our meals are breakfast, dinner, and then we have supper)

I'll share with you principles that if you apply any one of them, your skyrocketing grocery bill will go down noticeably. If you incorporate two or more, your bill will go down substantially. When all is said and done, it is my goal to help you cut your grocery bill in half.

I assure you, it is possible.

How would you feel if I told you it was possible to make over seventeen meals, out of an average bone-in ham?

Some time ago I was at a church supper, in which very high-end spiral hams were served. After the dinner I happened to walk by the kitchen where the cleanup committee was finishing up. I stopped dead in my tracks when I heard someone say, "Does anyone want to take the left over ham- bones home to his or her dog?" (Please don't get me wrong; I'm not against pets, but I know too many people that are struggling financially)

I went into the kitchen where at least ten ham bones with copious pieces of ham still attached, were sitting on the counter waiting to be disposed of. None of the women in the kitchen wanted them, so I said I would take them off their hands. They were glad to get them out of their way so they could finish cleaning up.

I personally knew of families that would welcome the hambone, as if they had won the lottery.

I gathered up all the hams and distributed them to the families who I knew would appreciate the bonanza. I took one home and began slicing the ham off the bone. My husband, in retelling this story to others always says, "We lived like Champs on the leftovers."

I filled a quart sized freezer bag (4 cups) with enough diced ham to make Scalloped Potatoes, Omelets, Creamy Wild Rice & Ham Soup and Potato Klub. I then boiled the bone, and made a large pot of Ham & Beans.

Using a pan and one cup of the diced **ham**, I made Scalloped Potatoes, which turned out to be more than enough for our family of three. The next day for lunch, my husband was able to take some leftovers to work and I had a nice meal at home. 2 meals

The Omelets I made twice during the month. One-fourth cup of **ham** sautéed with onions, dried green peppers (if fresh are not available) and dried mushrooms with a little cheese grated for the inside, and to sprinkle on the top. Serve with whole-wheat toast and you will have a difficult time in eating an entire omelet. One omelet fed three of us. 2 meals

Creamy Wild Rice & Ham soup is one of our family's favorite soups during the winter. If you used a cup of diced **ham** in a stockpot, it would make enough soup for the first meal, and enough left over to freeze for three more meals. Minimum of 4 meals

 Potato Klub is a Norwegian dish made mainly out of potatoes, and one recipe makes 8 balls. Flour and grated fresh potatoes are mixed together into a ball, and the one and one-half cup of diced **ham** and onions are pushed into the middle and then boiled.

We eat them after they have cooled down. I like to slice them very thin and fry the slices until crisp in butter for breakfast, usually with a couple of over-easy eggs. Our family of three uses two balls (depending on the size of the balls you make) for each breakfast. 4 meals

The ham bone, which still had meat left on it, I then placed into a stockpot to make ham and bean soup. We had this soup for supper and with what was leftover, filled four-quart sized bags to freeze for future days. 5 meals

So let's do the math. How many meals did we get out of a ham that someone was going to throw to Fido?

- One cup diced ham in the Scalloped Potatoes – 2 Meals
- One-fourth cup times 2 of ham - Omelets – 2 Meals
- One cup diced ham for the Wild Rice & Ham Soup – 4 Meals
- One and one-half cup diced ham for Potato Klub – 4 Meals
- Ham and Beans – 5 Meals

That totals 17 meals!

Notice that I haven't even mentioned the initial ham dinner, where the entire ham was cooked. Then there are the leftover ham slices that we placed in freezer bags, to be used for grilled ham & cheese sandwiches later on down the road. (Serve with your favorite soup of course)

This is the principle of "divide and multiply." It doesn't matter if we're talking about a turkey, beef roast or a chicken. (Check Lesson 15 on how to make five meals out of one chicken)

Be creative. Notice that in most of these meals, meat was not the main focus.

There is a paradigm shift that needs to take place in our lives concerning the use of meat. Unfortunately many make meat the focus of their three meals a day. (I'm assuming you live in a country where you are fortunate enough to have three meals a day) In fact, meat should be used sparingly, or even as flavoring to enhance the meal.

I am not advocating that you become a vegetarian. What I am saying is that because of the price of meat, (and it's going higher) we need to change our habits. Using these survival skills can stretch your food dollar, and give you peace of mind.

This journey will take work on your part, if you decide to follow any of these principles, but I promise you, it will be worth it.

* * * * *

Creamy Wild Rice & Ham Soup

¾ cup wild rice
1 Tablespoon olive oil
4 cups water
1 medium carrot, diced
1 large onion, chopped
1 or 2 celery stalks, diced
½ cup butter
½ cup flour
3 cups chicken broth
2 cups Half & Half or evaporated milk
1 cup **Ham**, diced
½ tsp. rosemary
¼ tsp. pepper
½ tsp. salt

I usually make soup in a stockpot. Any large kettle will do. Turn your stove onto medium heat, and sauté the rice in the olive oil for 5 minutes.

Add the water and salt and bring to a boil. Once it comes to a boil, turn the heat down, cover and simmer for 35 minutes. Drain into a sieve, reserving the water in a separate bowl.

In the kettle you simmered the rice, sauté the onion, celery and carrot in the butter until the onion is transparent.

Reduce heat; stir in flour and cook until bubbly. Gradually stir in the chicken broth and the liquid you reserved, stirring at all times.

Bring to a boil; boil for 2 minutes. Continue stirring.
Add half & half, ham, rosemary, pepper & rice.

Reduce heat; cover and simmer for 30-35 minutes or until rice is tender. (This should make enough for 8 servings or two quarts.}

How to make your soup last for more than two meals:

If you decide to have a sandwich with your soup it will extend the soup even further.

When the soup has cooled, pour three cups into a quart sized freezer bag and place in the refrigerator overnight. Make sure you squeeze the extra air out of the freezer bag as you seal it. In the morning place the bags flat on a cookie sheet and place in the freezer. Do not stack so they can freeze faster. Once they are frozen, remove the bags from the cookie sheet and stack in your freezer. Be sure to put a date and label each bag. You can also use freezer safe containers.

You now have soup that can be taken out and reheated when the kids come home, and inform you of a ball game you weren't planning on.

Scalloped Potatoes

Some people make scalloped potatoes using raw potatoes, and others will use leftover baked potatoes. My personal preference is using raw potatoes even though the cooking time is longer.

Having said that, today I am making scalloped potatoes with some large baked potatoes, which were left over from supper yesterday. I had filled the oven with potatoes with the intent of also putting up hash browns. But guess what? I lost track of the time, as it was apple-pressing time yesterday so the potatoes turned out to be great for eating, but too soft for making hash browns.

So here's what I did.

I peeled eight of the baked potatoes and sliced them into a buttered cake pan. I then sprinkled 1 cup of chopped ham over the top.

I remembered that the other day I had opened a can of milk just to use two tablespoons in some frosting. So in a bowl I mixed all that was left in the can, plus a cup of water, to two cans of cream-of-mushroom soup. I like spicy food so I wondered how a can of green chilies would taste in the mixture. Nailed it!

I then added to the mixture a cup of grated Parmesan cheese, ½ teaspoon salt and ½ teaspoon pepper. After mixing all that together I poured it over the potatoes & ham. I then added another cup of grated cheese to the top. Covered it with aluminum foil and baked it for 45 minutes at 350°.

Ham & Bean Soup

Left over **Ham bone**
2 large onion, diced
3 Cloves Garlic, minced
3 Tablespoons Butter
4 cups White Beans (Most people like Great Northern, some like Lima.)
6 cups Chicken Broth
4 cups water
2 cups diced potatoes
1 ½ cups carrots, diced
1 ½ cups celery, diced
1 cup frozen peas
½ tsp. pepper
3 Tablespoons parsley, minced (Fresh if you have it, or 2 Tablespoons dried)
Quart size freezer bags

Soak beans overnight. Over medium heat place the butter, onion and garlic in a large stockpot and sauté until the onion is transparent. If your family does not like diced onions, place the onions in the soup whole and remove them before serving. (Serve them to the person in the family who likes onions.) Add liquids, ham bone, beans and other vegetables, except the frozen peas and parsley. Cook until the vegetables are tender. For the last five minutes add the peas and parsley. Remove the ham bone and serve the soup with corn bread or any kind of bread your family likes. (Now you can give the ham bone to Fido) We usually find a corn bread recipe and serve that with butter and honey. Awesome!!! This recipe should make around 4 quarts of soup.

After your meal is over and the soup has cooled down, pour 3 cups of soup into each freezer bag (Make sure excess air is removed) and place them in the refrigerator overnight. In the morning lay them flat (Do not stack) on a cookie sheet and put into the freezer. Be sure to label and date each bag.

When they are frozen, remove them from the cookie sheet and stack in your freezer for future meals.

Ham and Vegetable Omelet

¼ cup chopped **Ham**
2 Tbs. olive oil (or your choice)
1 medium onion, diced, you could also use scallions or chives
1 cup diced zucchini (yellow and green if you want more color)
¼ cup pitted Kalamata olives or your choice of green olives. Do not go out and buy this ingredient if it is not in your pantry.
Six eggs (whipped)
¼ cup feta cheese (Once again, use whatever you have on hand)
½ cup shredded Parmesan cheese (or your favorite)
Salt and pepper to taste

In a cast iron skillet heat olive oil on medium heat and sauté onion, zucchini and olives for a few minutes. You don't want your vegetables to be over cooked. Remove from skillet into to a bowl and reserve until the eggs are cooked.

31

Whip your eggs until frothy and pour into the skillet you used for the vegetables. Cook one side and then carefully flip. On one half of the turned over eggs add the cooked vegetables, ham and feta cheese. Gently bring the egg half without the vegetable on so that it covers the vegetables. Sprinkle ½ cup of shredded cheese over the omelet and cover only until cheese is melted. Serve right away. This will serve three people if served with toast and juice. Add hash browns as a side if you have an extra hungry teenager.

Lesson Three ~ Fail to Plan, Plan to Fail!

I promised you that you could cut your food bill substantially if you followed certain principles.

First of all, nothing great is accomplished without a plan.

There are four things you can do that will guarantee immediate success in lowering your food expenditures.

Some time ago I was explaining to a gentleman what "Putting Up With Leona" was all about. When I came to the part about cutting one's food bill in half, he became so animated I almost thought he was going to jump over the top of his desk.

"This is exactly what our family needs," he exclaimed. "My family of four spends over seven hundred dollars a month on groceries and that doesn't include eating out."

I have to admit that my jaw dropped as I ran through my mind what my house would look like if I had seven hundred dollars a month to spend on groceries. I could see all the stacks of food I would have to navigate through to get to my kitchen. Then there would be the extra sheds going up in the back yard to accommodate the growing surplus.

He went on to say that even though he knew many of the reasons why they were spending so much, they hadn't as a family been able to sit down and formulate a plan.

This gentleman is not alone in his dilemma. And he hit the nail right on the head. You have to have a plan.

I shared with him the "Reader's Digest" condensed version of what I am about to share with you.

In the beginning, the following four principles will take some time on your part, but in the end, it will save you a great amount of time and expense.

First: Take time to go through your cupboards, freezer, pantry and fridge, and do a written inventory of what you do have in your home.

Please get rid of food items that your grandmother's great grandmother passed on to you. Chances are if you haven't used those items by now, you probably are not going to use them.
Defrost your freezer to make sure there is nothing lurking in the bottom, which may have petrified. When you purchase new items, the

old will go on top or to the front, depending whether you have an upright or chest freezer.

Now that you know what you have in your pantry, freezer, fridge and cupboards, you can move on to the next principle.

Second: Plan your meals for the next week. While a good goal to strive for is a month at a time, we will start out by planning a menu for one week.

Baby steps!

Unless you live alone, this is not a step you should take by yourself. Your entire family should be involved in this process. Everyone has their favorites and if they take  ownership in the choosing, they will be less likely to complain when a meal is served that they are not interested in.

BY THE WAY PEOPLE!!!!! You are not running a restaurant. If you are getting up every morning and asking your children what they want for breakfast, or it's five o'clock in the evening and you want to know what everyone wants for supper, you are setting yourself up for stress, picky eaters and rotten kids. (Did I say that out loud?)

My mother-in-law had a sign on her fridge that made her life very simple.

"Today's menu choice, TAKE IT or LEAVE IT."

Ideally, I have found one of the best ways to plan the meals with the family is to sit down together Sunday afternoon, evening, or any time that works for you, and have a family council.

You should come to this meeting armed with four things,

✓ Knowledge of what is already in your storage.
✓ Sale flyers for the week from local grocery stores. (One for each person if possible)
✓ A large calendar or paper for writing the menu on. (To be posted on the fridge)
✓ A piece of paper that will be your shopping list.

Not only does calling a family council give everyone in the family the opportunity to choose a meal, but you also find out what is happening during the upcoming week, that will effect whether or not you will be eating supper together on a particular evening. Then the nights where school plays, games, meetings and other activities are scheduled will not come as a surprise to anyone.

Eating out should not be one of the menu choices if you are trying to cut back on your grocery budget. Make the crockpot your best friend on those busy days. Once again, 'If you fail to plan, you plan to fail."

Another amazing thing about having a menu is that you will notice you wrote it on a calendar or a piece of paper, not stone, so therefore it is flexible.

Because you planned ahead and have all the ingredients in your home for the entire week, you will be able to deal with surprises like unexpected company, or events that may not have been talked about in your family council. The spaghetti supper you planned for Thursday, will go farther than the tacos you planned for Monday, (the night that one of your children decides to bring home a friend). There will be no need to run to the store to accommodate the added mouth to feed.

So using the input of your family, your knowledge of what is already in your home for groceries, and using the weekly grocery store flyers, you have enough input to plan your menu.

Try this exercise. Write down the meals you cook in a two-week period. Studies show that after a certain age most people quit adding to their vocabulary. The same holds true with regards to the meals we eat from day to day.

Many people eat the same twelve or so meals over and over. So it might help to come up with what those meals are in your family, and include those on your menu on a rotating basis. It would definitely make your grocery shopping a breeze.

However, just like adding a new word to your vocabulary would expand your horizons, a new recipe every month would greatly add to the fun of family dinners.

You may want to come up with clever ways to display your weekly menu. I have seen some people place an artsy weekly menu in framed glass, and then hang it on a wall in the kitchen for all to see. This way you can use a marker to write on top of the glass, and erase it after each week.

Another fun way to display the menu is to hang a small chalkboard in your kitchen. Beware!!! Little munchkins may change a certain supper they don't like to something more to their liking. Maybe hiding the chalk would be in order.

Remember: A goal unwritten is only a wish!

During the family council meeting we talked about, I mentioned that you should have a shopping list to keep track of what items will be needed to make your menu possible.

Third: A shopping list. As you discuss the meals you want for the next week, write down the ingredients that are missing from your freezer and cupboards.

After your family planning session, make sure the shopping list along with your menu is displayed on the fridge or some other clever way for all to see.

I personally just find a favorite magnet and put my shopping list and menu on the fridge.

Your menu can be placed wherever you want to around the kitchen, but it's very important that the shopping list be on the fridge.

One of the things you want your family to get in the habit of doing is adding to the list. By that I don't mean adding whatever they might be craving at the moment. But whenever someone in the family finishes off the last bottle of ketchup, mayo or pickles, they should automatically add that item to the list.

It's aggravating to be making a cake only to find out that someone used the last of the cocoa last week on brownies. It will also save you another unnecessary trip to the grocery store.

Remember, every trip you make to the grocery store cuts into your budget. I don't know of anyone who walks into a store to pick up one item – and walks out of the store with just that one item.

Never, never, never and never go grocery shopping without your list.

So, armed with your list, you are ready to head out to the store.

Well, you might think you're ready, but are you really?

Four: Shopping. This takes a little more thought than getting in the car and driving on your merry way.
Let me share with you some of the shopping tips that students have brought up in my classes.

- ✓ Never go shopping when you are hungry. For all of us who have done this you know that everything in the store looks good. Strangely even things you would not normally buy.
- ✓ Pick a day that is not already full. If you are knee deep in alligators on the day you go shopping, it will be rushed and your hurried decision-making will affect your budget.
- ✓ Child care. There are two schools of thought on this. Some in the classes said they would never take their children grocery shopping with them. In that case, try to find someone you can trade childcare with so that you do not have that added expense. The second thought is to use the shopping trip as an opportunity to teach your children how to shop themselves. They also learn that they can't have everything they see and that each item has a price.

I remember when our youngest son was four. We were shopping and were about to check out at the counter. He saw the beef jerky that was so conveniently displayed at his level, and removed it from the shelf.

He asked me if he could have it because he really, really wanted it. We were on an extremely tight budget at the time, (you know the "chicken today and feathers tomorrow" budget, except we were on the feathers part) but I told him that, 'yes, he could have it, if he wanted to go home and get the change he had in his piggy bank and pay for it himself."

He looked at the jerky for a few seconds and mumbled under his breath, as he put it back on the shelf, "I'm not spending "my" money on it." No tantrum, just the logical conclusion that items in the grocery store are not free.

In lesson three, we talked about the gentleman who confessed that his family spent over seven hundred dollars a month on groceries.

He probably spends more than that, so let's cut down his budget to four hundred a month.

So now, we are heading out the door with one hundred dollars in an envelope in our possession, along with our shopping list. Do NOT use a charge card or debit card for groceries. Having real money in your hand makes it a little more painful and real, as you hand it over.

More than likely you will not spend the entire amount. The extra will be for in-store items that were not advertised, that you might want to use to begin building food storage.

If the produce manager, during blueberry season, wants to unload his overstock of blueberries at 99 cents a pint, you will want to buy ten. When you take them home and put them in freezer bags, you'll have enough for muffins and pancakes all winter long.

If you do not spend the entire hundred, be sure to keep it in your grocery envelope, and carry it over to the next week's budget.

Some of you may not like this next word of advice.

"Get over being loyal to brands!"

Notice how I made it flowery, so it would be easier to handle?
Since we make our own bread, I very rarely buy it, but when I do, I always think back on the time when my husband and I worked at a large bakery.

A truck pulled back into the dock with an order that had been rejected at a local store, because it was not the right brand. The supervisor, after expressing his frustration in a colorful manner, told us to unload all the bread, remove the wrappers, and replace them with the brand wrapper the store had requested. The one requested, of course, was much more expensive. This is not an isolated incident in factories and cannery's.

These four principles; Taking an inventory, planning a menu, using your shopping list and purposeful shopping, will drastically cut down on what you spend on food each week.

Happy shopping!

Inventory

Freezer

- ❖ _____
- ❖ _____
- ❖ _____
- ❖ _____
- ❖ _____
- ❖ _____
- ❖ _____
- ❖ _____
- ❖ _____
- ❖ _____
- ❖ _____
- ❖ _____
- ❖ _____

Pantry / Cupboards

- ❖ _____
- ❖ _____
- ❖ _____
- ❖ _____
- ❖ _____
- ❖ _____
- ❖ _____
- ❖ _____
- ❖ _____
- ❖ _____
- ❖ _____
- ❖ _____
- ❖ _____

Menu

Monday
Breakfast -
Dinner -
Supper –

Tuesday
Breakfast -
Dinner -
Supper –

Wednesday
Breakfast -
Dinner -
Supper –

Thursday
Breakfast -
Dinner -
Supper –

Friday
Breakfast -
Dinner -
Supper –

Saturday
Breakfast -
Dinner -
Supper –

Sunday
Breakfast -
Dinner -
Supper –

Shopping List

❖ _____
❖ _____
❖ _____
❖ _____
❖ _____
❖ _____
❖ _____
❖ _____
❖ _____
❖ _____
❖ _____
❖ _____
❖ _____
❖ _____
❖ _____
❖ _____
❖ _____
❖ _____

Lesson Four ~ Food Storage, Not a Bad Idea!

"Come, ye thankful people come;
Raise the song of harvest home.
All is safely gathered in
Ere the winter storms begin."
~Henry Alford, 1810-1871

It's October and I am exhausted, but it's the kind of exhaustion that feels good.

The potatoes are all dried and stored in the basement. The onions are drying on the tarp in the driveway. The garden is spread with manure and tilled under. The apples are all pressed, and jars filled with fresh apple juice.

The only thing left calling my name is the horseradish, which we'll do when the temperature goes down a little more.

I also haven't had time to make raspberry jam, but all the raspberries are frozen and when things slow down, it will be jamming time.

Having the pantry full is a good feeling. People, for some reason, don't seem to stock up for winter like they used to.

In the introduction of this book I shared with you my memories of visiting my grandparent's home. I would sit on the basement steps just so I could look at all the shelves of canning my grandmother had put up for the winter. The colors of the cherries, peaches, pears, pickled beets, watermelon pickles and a myriad of others products, reminded me of opening a new box of crayons on the first day of school.

My Grandparents lived five miles out of town, and often, in the winter, they would be homebound for weeks at a time. There was no running to the store if Grandma should run out of some ingredient.

That wasn't an option, and it just didn't happen. They could live all winter on what they had put up.

They didn't call it "Food Storage." It was their way of life, and it was just common sense to be prepared for any major storm that would come their way.

When you live in the Midwest, it's not "if" a storm will happen. It's when! Alberta Clippers are a given.

It really doesn't matter what area of the country you live in, being prepared for "events" in one's life is not a bad idea.

During the seventies, while living in Alaska, there was a trucker's strike. At that time, most of Alaska's commodities arrived by containers on barges or by trucks driving the Alcan. When the strike was announced, what do you think immediately disappeared from the local stores? I know you just said bread and milk, and that's what I would have said also. Not so. It was toilet paper! Houdini could not have done a better disappearing act.

The old sourdoughs that had lived in Alaska most of their lives, knew that you always kept a winters supply in the old cache to survive.

In this day and age, the weather reporting has become pretty sophisticated. They can almost tell you the exact day, and time of the day, that a storm will arrive.

One winter, when we were living in Boston, a Nor-Easter was forecast. Once again, every convenience store and local grocery chain was emptied of milk and bread. If you waited to pick up those items on your way home from work, you were just out of luck.

I think one of the most amazing "run of the unprepared" I have ever witnessed, was while we were living in Hawaii, and a hurricane was about to bear down on the islands.

I want you to know this is not an exaggeration. When the weather station first announced that the storm was definite, to the time the shelves in the stores were totally empty, was 30 minutes.

The first thing to go was Spam. That happens to be a staple in Hawaii and you have to have lived there or at least visited, to know how important Spam is to the Hawaiians.

Just before Hurricane Sandy hit the East Coast we were visiting our son in New York City. He and his wife live in a small brownstone apartment.

One of the things that concerned us was that there wasn't enough food in the house to fix meals for one day. Their life style is such that they eat out all the time. We encouraged them to put at least a week's supply of food in the kitchen, to cover any emergencies that may come up.

More a less our dear children told us not to worry ourselves. They both work at restaurants, so they would be covered. The week after we left, Sandy hit. Everything in New York shut down.

We that live in the Midwest have several examples of our own.

All someone has to say is, "Why I remember back in the winter of "96-97"when...... And everyone will nod their head and eagerly wait their turn to tell their "survival" story.

The wisdom of having food storage covers many more events, which you may not have considered. A disaster can be anything that disrupts our lives from what we are comfortable with.

During a class on "Starting a Food Storage" we came up with several reasons why having storage would be prudent.

Factory shutdowns; strikes, downsizing at work, hours cutback temporally, and one spouse losing their job when you have become dependent on the income of both paychecks, were some of the most obvious reasons.

Medical events can be another common reason, accompanied with its skyrocketing bills.

Divorce or death of a spouse will cause a great deal of stress. No brainer!!

Not to mention holding down a job while furthering your education.

How about stores pulling food items because of being tainted?

Very, very few of us are living today that would remember the flu of 1918 and what it did to the American people, and the world. All public events were cancelled and stores even closed their doors.

Through all these stressful events, you have to eat. And that's where your food storage comes in.

Don't be overwhelmed! And don't do anything stupid, like rush out and purchase a year's supply of food. Yes, we need to be prepared for the unsettling events that come our way, but we also need to use common sense in the way we prepare.

Remember the "Millennium" Y2K bug that got everyone in an uproar? Not to mention bird flu, salmonella scares, and all the other scare tactics that seem to permeate the media. What did people do? Well, they ran out and spent millions of dollars on food storage, so they could be prepared for an event that was not as catastrophic as forecasted. Be wise!

Should we be prepared for unseen events? Absolutely, but let's do it in a sensible way. So, let's get started.

In Lesson Three, I shared with you the importance and the simplicity of planning a weekly menu. That weekly menu will be our starting point for building a month's supply of food storage.

The menu you planned has seven days of meals that you know your family will eat, because they helped you plan it.

So **first**, take that menu and fill in the rest of the month, duplicating the same menu for each of the remaining three weeks. You now have your meals planned for a month.

If you have a two-week menu planned, you can duplicate the next two weeks of the month with the same menu. Voila! You now have the first step completed, that will help you towards a short-term goal of a month's food supply.

The **second** step is to recalculate your shopping list, to reflect what is needed to fix meals for the entire month.

Yes, you will need to revisit the store for perishable items such as fresh fruits and vegetables, but you now have your main items in your pantry and freezer.

The **third** step requires you to keep your eyes open for items that go on sale, that may not be on your shopping list. For example, if there is an unadvertised in-store special on ketchup for 89 cents a bottle, it would be a smart thing to purchase several at that price. Since you have already taken an inventory of what you have at home, you know what items need to be added to.

Let me share with you some basic items you might want to consider storing. I am assuming that you don't plan all your meals from a can or box mix. If you don't know how to bake simple items (like a cake or pancakes) from scratch, you need to learn.

Later we will be talking about making your own mixes. (Such as, pancake, tortilla, and salad dressings) Remember any mix you see in the store was made in the home first.

These basic items, which you will need in your storage, will help you stretch your food dollar, and keep you from running to the store.

Powdered & canned milk: Okay, so the first thing you are going to say is, "My family will not drink powdered milk. I don't want to hear it. Even if they won't drink it, powdered milk can be used in all your recipes that call for milk.

When my children were small, and the store-bought gallon of milk would reach the halfway mark, I would make two quarts of non-instant powdered milk, and fill the milk container, so that it was full again. I found that as long as the non-instant powdered milk was mixed the night before so that it was cold the next morning, they never knew the difference.

Salt: This will be one of your most inexpensive items to purchase, so make it your first item on the list. Even if you bake every day, one 1-pound box of salt would be more than enough for a month's supply.

Oil/lard: Pick what your family likes, whether it is extra-virgin olive oil, canola, sunflower, vegetable, or any of the oils available at the store. I choose to store fresh rendered lard, and extra-virgin olive oil.

Once a year we gather up the pig fat from butchering, and render it down into beautiful white lard. We do most of our baking, like pies, cookies and mixes with this lard. If you want to do this, just visit your local butcher, and ask if he will save the fat for you. After rendering it down, we store it in the freezer or the extra fridge in the garage.

Many years ago, I had a friend who had lived in Germany after World War II. She shared with me a story I have never forgotten.

Many Germans were starving. They would gather wild garlic, or anything else edible. But one item in demand that turned you into a wealthy person, was whether or not you had cooking oil in your home. Oil was money, and you could trade it for anything else that was available.

Dry grains & legumes: The list on this is endless. Just make sure you store what your family likes. These items store for a longer time period. Barley, pasta products, rice, flour, cornmeal, rolled oats, dry beans, (pink, kidney, lima, pinto, chickpeas, great northern, split peas,

to name a few) and wheat are things you may want to think about. These items should be stored in gallon containers or plastic buckets that seal well.

Sugar/honey: The thing about storing sugar is that even though it may harden, it does not affect the quality of the sugar. If you would rather store honey, the same principle applies. If it crystalizes, all you have to do is place the container in a pan of hot water (not boiling) and it will melt into a liquid again.

Water: Several weeks ago, without any notice from the city, everyone's water was shut off so they could clean out the hydrants. It would have been nice to have some warning but it didn't happen. Not to worry! I had enough water stored for washing hands, brushing our teeth and flushing the toilet (pour the dishwater when you are finished doing dishes) during the day. We even had water for boiling spaghetti for dinner.

During the winter we have melted snow when water mains froze, so we could carry on with our daily routine. (Side bar; indoor plants love water from melted snow)

These six suggestions will help you in your quest to be self-reliant.

Do not go out and buy everything you would like to put up in your storage at once.

Do it in a systematic and logical method that won't jeopardize your food budget.

Today is a good day to start. I like what Moses said to the Israelite's after he explained to them what was expected of them. "Hear therefore, O Israel, and observe to <u>do it</u>; that it may be well with thee, and that ye may increase mightily...."

Sounds like timeless counsel to me.

Lesson Five ~ Fast Foods

Fast Food! "I do not think that means what you think that means. I have heard on many occasions, which the American English language is one of the most confusing and most difficult languages to learn. I say American, because the British accuse us of not speaking English at all.

Let's take the word "fast" as an example.

You may for one reason or another be holding a "fast," which of course means you are abstaining from all food for a specific amount of time.

If you pull "a fast one" on someone, you have just played an unfair trick on them.

I may encourage you to "hold fast", thereby encouraging you to be tenacious in what you know to be right.

When you ask me if the baby was sleeping, I wouldn't say, "Yes, she is in a deep and sound sleep." I would probably say she is "fast asleep."

The dictionary had 27 various meanings of the word fast.

The one we are going to focus on is definition #2 which states, "something that is done in a comparatively little or short time."

Recently, after a wonderful brunch, our family took an unplanned drive around town to take in the beautiful fall foliage. We were not in the car for an hour, when my four-year-old grandson proclaimed to all, that he wanted to stop for some "Fast Food."

What he was really saying is, "I'm hungry, and I want something to eat right now!"

To his disappointment, his mother was way ahead of the situation, and told him that she had "fast food" waiting for him at home. Of course that was not the kind of fast food he was talking about, but she stuck to her guns in spite of some weeping, wailing, and gnashing of teeth on our grandson's part.

A very short time later we were back home, and she pulled out food that she had prepared in advance, for times when she needed a meal in a comparatively short time.

Now, she didn't pull out a frozen TV dinner or some pre-fab food that had been fixed in some factory. The meals she had stored in her freezer were of her own making, and I might say, have helped cut the grocery budget considerably. Not to mention eliminating the stress level factor that arises, when small children or teenagers want food right now, or they will surely die.

So here's the process. Simply put...whenever you make a meal, make more than you need.

For example, if you are making lasagna, you are already going through all the steps to assemble all the ingredients, why not set two pans in front of you and make two at one time?

I usually make lasagna in a cake pan. It doesn't seem to take any more time to make two instead of just one and if you really feel ambitious, you could make more than two.

Usually a family does not finish off an entire pan of lasagna in one meal, so the leftover lasagna is divided into sectioned containers to take to work.

Leftovers! We will talk about those later also.

The same rule applies when you make spaghetti sauce. Make a stockpot full. Feed your family for the evening meal and then when it cools down, divide the remainder into quart freezer bags for later use. Making a huge pot of spaghetti sauce, to me, is one of the best time savers. This sauce can be used in making your lasagna, pizza and other spaghetti dinners.

Recently I made an enormous pot of stir-fry for supper. Using one cup of diced chicken as flavoring and by adding a copious amount of vegetables, I was able to put up three, quart size freezer bags into the freezer. Heating up stir-fry for another meal down the road when you are stressed for time is really "fast food."

Why is cooking more than you need for one meal a really smart idea?

How many times have you been called on to take a meal over to someone who is sick, or had an accident, or one of the many other reasons where someone may need your help?

Service to others never comes at a convenient time does it? Usually it comes when your day is already full. And usually the help is needed immediately.

Because you put up extra meals in your freezer, you have just undermined a potentially stressful situation. Take that lasagna and a loaf of bread out of the freezer, whip up a salad, and you are out the door.

What about your own emergencies? You didn't plan the day you are going to get the flu, or break an arm. But when an emergency does strike, you are prepared with meals that your family can take out of the freezer, and put in the oven at the end of the day.

When they bring you supper in bed and proudly say, "Look what we made for you," just weakly smile and say how grateful you are for their thoughtfulness. Your planning ahead paid off big time.

What about tacos? Fry up several pounds of hamburger, or other meat, when you fix a taco meal. Once again, as soon as the meat has cooled down, put it up in containers for future "fast food" meals on days when your family is on the go.

All soups freeze well. You don't think the soup you get in your local restaurant is homemade do you? Very rarely! Much of it is frozen in bags, shipped to the restaurant and thawed out. So you are paying around eight dollars to have them thaw out soup that was made who knows how long ago, heat it up, so you can have the illusion that you are back in grandma's cozy kitchen on a cold winters day.

Do it yourself! Create your own coziness, by always making more soup than you can eat in one meal and put the rest up. You won't regret it.

Once again, these are only a few of the ways in which you can create your own fast food. Think about your family's favorite meals, and be creative in how you can plan for those busy days or evenings, where someone says, "Can we go out for fast food tonight?"

"Ha!!!" you say, "Coming right up, in a comparatively short time."

* * * * *

Basic Spaghetti Sauce

This sauce can be used for spaghetti dinner, pizza, lasagna, pizza bagels, or any recipe that calls for a tomato-based sauce.

1 pound hamburger
1 pound spicy Italian sausage
Six large mushrooms sliced thin
1 large onion, diced
Six quarts of canned tomatoes
Four pints of tomato sauce
2 – 12 oz. cans tomato paste
Six toes of garlic, pressed (to taste)
2 Tablespoons parsley flakes
2 tsp. salt
2 Tablespoons sugar
¼ cup Italian seasoning spice **OR** add the following spices;
2 Tablespoons oregano
1 Tablespoon rosemary
1 Tablespoon thyme
2 Tablespoons basil
Six bay leaves
½ tsp. crushed red pepper flakes (optional)

In a stockpot, or any large pot you need to sauté hamburger, sausage, mushrooms and onions. If your family does not like chunky sauce, blend the canned tomatoes in your blender. Then add to the meat. Add all the remaining ingredients. Read the recipe over first, so that you are aware that you either use Italian Seasoning spice or the four spices mentioned afterwards.

Simmer for one hour or until it is the thickness you like it. If it is not thick enough for you, mix 2 Tablespoons of cornstarch into as much water and drizzle into the sauce while you are stirring.

With what is left over after your spaghetti dinner, cool down, and divide into freezer bags for future meals. If you are freezing the sauce for pizza, you will want to freeze ½ cup in individual containers.
For recipes that call for a small amount of sauce, use ice cube trays.

Lesson Six ~ Breakfast

IF it's true what they say that, "breakfast is the most important meal of the day", THEN how on earth did we come up with the notion that breakfast had to consist of such boring and unsavory items as sugary cold cereals, pastries, or rubbery waffles taken from cellophane wrappers and plopped into the toaster?

My mother-in-law always told her children if they tried to rush off to school without eating, "You're not leaving this house without breakfast." She made sure they ate a hearty, stick to your ribs breakfast. Oh, they ate cold cereal, but it was always on weekends when they were home, that way they could eat a half hour later when the cereal wore off.

While visiting relatives with small children some time ago, I was shocked to find out that you can buy just about anything already cooked, sealed in packages, and ready to heat up in a moment's notice. As I read *some* of the ingredients on these packages, I realized I could not pronounce over half the items listed. My rule is "If you need a pharmaceutical degree to read the ingredients on a food package, don't eat it."

Who do you think convinced Western society that sending a child off to school on a cold winter's morning with a bowl of cold cereal, was sufficient to stick to those little ribs until lunch? The prophet Isaiah said it well – "All we like sheep!" (Isaiah 53:6)

Many years ago my husband drove the school bus. He would come home shaking his head at the number of children who got on the bus with a can of pop in one hand and a toaster pastry in the other. Can you imagine those children, around 10 o'clock in the morning, coming down off that sugar high?

I know we are all in a hurry to get out the door in the morning. We grab whatever is easy, stuff it down and take off running. Stop it!!!

Our children deserve better than that and so do you. With a little bit of planning on our part, we can turn hectic mornings into pleasant experiences.

First of all let me share with you some of my favorite things to eat for breakfast.

 A BLT on whole-wheat toast! Whenever I buy a package of bacon on sale, I fry it up and keep it in a container in the fridge. (An added benefit is the lard left over from frying a pound of bacon, can be stored in small containers for frying) It then takes much less time to make the BLT as I already have the bacon fried. I can also use one piece of bacon, crumbled up to add to my pancake batter, French toast, scrambled eggs, muffins or even a baked potato. Amazing time saver!

On a cold winter's Midwest morning, try a grilled cheese sandwich with a bowl of soup. Now this isn't just any old can of soup. This is soup that you saved from the stockpot full you made the week before and divided into small breakfast size portions and put up in the freezer. It will have amazing results on your children's disposition.

When you make waffles on a Saturday morning, make a huge batch of batter and use the extra to make waffles for the freezer. (If you want to, add one slice of crisp cooked and crumbled bacon to the batter for flavoring) Then you have your own toaster waffles for those busy days.

Who says that you can't have that left over pizza, tacos or even lasagna from the night before? Pizza re-heated is awesome for breakfast. Little tummies are happy, when they leave the house with something warm inside them.

Breakfast can be totally different in the summer. This is where I really cut back on the meat, and eat it sparingly. Meat keeps your body warm, and is best eaten in winter. So you may want to consider a breakfast of fruit only, yogurt with granola, poached eggs on toast, scrambled eggs, muffins with bacon pieces & shredded cheese mixed in, cinnamon bread sliced and made into French toast, homemade cinnamon buns, homemade creamy malted wheat or fried potatoes with over-easy eggs. So, thinking outside the box, breakfast encompasses a greater variety than we had considered before.

One member of my family makes the most fantastic biscuits and gravy when we visit. This is ready at any given morning, no matter how busy, because she makes a huge batch of sausage gravy ahead of time, divides it into several meals and freezes it. You can  also make the biscuits in advance and freeze them. You would swear, by the taste, that she had just spent all morning in the kitchen making everything fresh.

Here is a quick and easy recipe for "Creamy Malted Wheat." The only extra items you will want to keep on hand for this, is a container of dry malted milk and whole-wheat flour. This is a very inexpensive and comforting hot morning meal.

* * * * *

Creamy Malted Wheat

2 cups cold Water
1 tablespoon Butter
1 heaping tablespoon Malt
2 Tablespoons brown sugar
½ cup whole-wheat flour
Dash of salt

Mix above ingredients in a medium saucepan and stir with a wire whisk. Place over medium heat and continue to stir until mixture is thick. Usually, around five minutes as whole-wheat flour takes longer to cook. If too thick, add more water.   Serve with honey or brown sugar. Top with small amount of milk. Whole-wheat toast is excellent with this.

I don't know why, but every time I fix this, my tummy feels really happy.

So the bottom line is, don't be a "sheeple" and be misdirected into thinking there are only certain things you can eat for breakfast.

Lesson Seven ~ Waste Not, Want Not

Now some people attribute this saying to "Benny the Frank" around 1772, but if you check back in history, the saying went like this; "willful waste makes woeful want."

Truth be known, it doesn't take a MIT degree to figure out that if you don't waste what you are privileged enough to have, down the road, you won't have to wish you hadn't wasted it. Once again, no brainer!

One can safely assume that this principle has been around from the beginning of time. Unfortunately, it is mostly forgotten during the prosperity portion of the prosperity/want cycle.

"Waste Not, Want Not," is a major principle in cutting our grocery bill down. In fact I would say it's a major player.

This brings up a word that most people find distasteful;

"LEFTOVERS"!!!!

A few years ago, a neighbor of mine stopped over to complain that she didn't have anything thawed out for the evening meal, and had decided to call her husband who worked in town, to bring home some meat for supper.

As she tried to figure out what kind of meat she wanted him to pick up, she went over the last two days meals with me (pork chops and roast) and decided she would have him pick up a chicken.

I asked her if she had leftovers from those two meals in her fridge.

To which she replied, as she wrinkled up her nose, "Oh, my family won't eat leftovers."

I wanted to tell her to call 1-800-whaah, but I maintained my stoic mid-west demeanor and said, "Let's go take a look in your fridge and see what we can come up with."

An hour later, she sat at her kitchen table with an amazed look on her face, counting at least six meals made from "leftovers" that she would have thrown in the garbage.

The pork chops were used along with vegetables and rice to make a humongous pan of stir-fry. After using the stir-fry for the evening meal, she said her husband, who loved stir-fry, would take the remaining for his lunch the next day. (Even though it was "leftovers")

The leftover roast was used to make a huge pot of stew, which translated into four meals when divided into freezer bags for later use.

Nothing was thrown away, and she didn't have to ask her husband to stop on the way home to pick up something for supper.

Let's talk about the waste that goes on during the holidays.

Just the other day I was at an acquaintances home where I was helping with the clean up after supper. She had served turkey with all the trimmings. After I had separated all the loose turkey meat and removed what I could from the bones, I asked her what she wanted me to do with the carcass.

I knew she was going to say, "Throw it away." Yup, she did.

I was going take it home with me but instead I thought it might be a good time to teach her what a gold mine she was about to cast away.

I found her stockpot, filled it with water, broke up all the bones, scraped up left over drippings from the bottom of the roaster, and added them to the water. I ended up with six quarts of turkey stock, that could be used in soups, gravies, or any recipe that called for chicken stock.

Years ago we lived in Brazil for a year and a-half. One of the sounds that have never left me, as we walked down the streets, was the sound of the pressure cooker gauge, coming from almost every home. Beans and rice was a daily meal for most people in the region we were in.

The beans were on the stove by 11:30 and we would eat by noon.

I made up my mind upon returning to the States, that I would purchase a small pressure cooker, so I could use more dry beans and do it in the short time they did.

Well it's been a learning experience for me. Every bean seems to be different, and has a different cooking time.

One of my first batches of beans, which I cooked for only 15 minutes, was nothing but mush when I finally opened the pressure cooker. I wanted to make chili, but my chili recipe did not call for mushy beans.

In my younger years, I may have thrown them away. Instead, I went to plan B.

I put the beans into a cast iron skillet, mashed them up further with a potato masher, added the ingredients that are called for in re-fried beans, and divided the mixture into four portions. The next four times we had tacos, or burritos, I went to the freezer and pulled out my "bean mistake."

Refried Beans

1 pound pinto beans cooked and mashed
At least one cup of liquid reserved from boiling the beans
6 slices bacon
½ cup finely chopped onion
1 clove garlic, crushed
1 ½ tsp. salt
1 tsp. chili powder

Wash beans and cover with cold water in a large bowl. Refrigerate overnight.

The next day, pour beans and the liquid into a large stockpot, cover and boil until beans are tender.

Be sure to reserve at least a cup of liquid when you drain the beans. Mash the beans and set aside.

In a cast iron skillet, sauté the bacon until crisp. Drain on a paper towel and when cool, crumble. Use the bacon drippings to sauté the onion and garlic, for about 5 minutes.

With a wooden spoon, add the mashed beans, bacon, salt and chili powder to the onion and garlic.

Continue to cook over medium heat. If it becomes too thick, add little of the bean water you reserved.

Cool and divide into portion sizes that you think your family will eat in one meal. Spoon the portion sizes into freezer bags for future meals. Remember to write the date on each bag.

Another lifesaver for me is the ice cube tray. I usually buy lemons and limes in the 3-5 pound sacks. If I know that the recipes I have planned will not allow me to use them up quickly, I will zest the outside and place the zest in a freezer bag. Then I squeeze the juice into ice cube trays. When they are frozen, I remove them from the trays, and place them in freezer bags. I later will use them in Mexican dishes, salsa and fish recipes.

You might think that this is not worth your time, but during this last year I remember going to the store and for a few months, limes were over one dollar apiece. I could pass them by knowing that I had my stash in the freezer. Do the same with oranges.

Here in the Mid-West, we are used to eating green bananas. When mine get the smallest brown spot on the skin, to me it means they are over ripe. But, not to worry! They go directly into the freezer to be used later in cakes, muffins, bread, and smoothies. We haven't thrown out a banana in years.

Quoting "Benny the Frank" again, "If you know how to spend less than you get, you have the "Philosopher's Stone." Good old Benjamin Franklin, he knew what he was talking about.

I'm not sure why I never tire of the story of Joseph in Egypt and his ability to make "lemonade out of lemons" every time life handed him a new experience.

Now I'm not saying, (for those of you who are familiar with the story) that we are about to repeat the seven years of great plenty and the seven years of famine cycle, I am only saying we could learn a great deal from his experience.

You have to admit we live in a day of excess, plenty, abundance, and self-indulgence. Unfortunately, this also brings about the waste that we discussed earlier. We are a throwaway society, without any thought of the next day, much less giving thought to several months ahead, or even a year down the road.

In Joseph's case, he presented a seven-year food storage plan to the king of Egypt, to save his people from an upcoming disaster. We would be doing well if we would at least plan (as a starter) three months ahead.

Many of us experience overeating and waste that comes with holiday (Thanksgiving, Christmas, New Year's, and Easter) parties, I think it would be wise to continue our conversation on how to avoid waste.

These are a few of the ideas that have been dancing around in my head like visions of sugarplums.

November and December is the time to buy an extra turkey when they are so inexpensive. Get out the pressure cooker. Process it according to directions and you should be able to get around 24 quarts of turkey and broth that could be used in soups or any other favorite poultry recipes.

Every year after the 1st of January, I visit the produce manager at our  local store. It's a fact that the cranberries will sit there till the cows come home, so usually they will make a good deal with you to take the remainder of the cranberries off their hands. January is a wonderful time to put up cranberries for the rest of the year.

I never purchase croutons, seasoned breadcrumbs, stuffing mix or have I had to use my fresh bread for bread pudding in many moons. I have gotten in the habit of saving all my left over dinner rolls, end pieces of bread, or bread that has begun to dry out, and add them to a gallon freezer bag that I keep in the freezer.

Seasoned breadcrumbs are so easy to make in your blender, and they can also be either stored in the freezer or a glass container.

November and December is also a very convenient time of the year to make up what we used to call "TV" dinners. Most people use plastic containers now, so they can heat them up at work, or your children could have a nice hot meal after school. Just fill your divided plastic containers with left over mashed potatoes/gravy, a vegetable, some turkey or ham and there you go – no waste.

Speaking of vegetables, you will probably be making vegetable trays for super bowl games. Usually we cut up all those vegies and throw the trimmings away. Don't!!! Save all the trimmings from the celery, carrot, broccoli, cauliflower or whatever other vegetables you use, for future vegetable soup stock. Just keep a freezer bag in the freezer, and you can add to it and then use it up during the winter.

It might not be a bad idea to incorporate some of the wisdom of Joseph into our daily lives. Planning for the future always saves us stress, time and money.

* * * * *

Seasoned Bread Crumbs

For several months, or as long as it takes, I save the heels or pieces of bread that have dried out and put them in a zip-lock bag in the freezer. It doesn't matter if it's whole wheat, white or sourdough bread, I save it all.

When I have filled the gallon bag I take it out of the freezer and blend about one cup at a time and place in a large bowl until the entire gallon bag is blended. To the breadcrumbs add the following spices and mix thoroughly:

½ tsp. pepper
1 tsp. garlic powder
1 Tablespoon parsley flakes
½ tsp. salt
1 tsp. oregano
1 tsp. basil
1 tsp. onion powder

After the spices have been added, there are several ways you can make sure the crumbs are completely dry, as sometimes moisture gathers to the bread while it is in the freezer.

Place your mixture on a large cookie sheet and set in a warm place for a day or you could use your dehydrator. The oven set very low is another option. The dehydrator and the oven shorten the drying time. Your seasoned bread crumbs can be used for any recipe.

Spiced Cranberry Sauce

Whole Cranberries (enough to fill a 12 quart stock pot)
Sugar - 4 cups
Water
Zest from 2 oranges
2 cups Orange juice
½ tsp. cinnamon
1 tsp. ground nutmeg

Fill stockpot with whole cranberries, and then pour enough water in the pot to bring the level up to half of your cranberries. I usually add about 4 cups of sugar because I like my cranberries tart.

Add remaining ingredients.

Bring to a boil while stirring often has they burn easy, especially if you are using a stainless steel stockpot.

Once the mixture comes to a boil, turn the heat down to a gently rolling boil. When the mixture seems thick enough, pour into hot pint canning jars. I usually hot water bath the pint jar for ten minutes.

Lesson 8 ~ Potatoes

"One Potato, Two Potato,
Three Potato Four,
Five Potato. Six Potato,
Seven Potato, More,"

Its winter as I write this, and the weather outside is frightful, but I have to tell you why inside my house is so delightful. Simply put, Potatoes! Or should I say the smell of "potato soup."

It is January, and the potatoes we gleaned in the fall, that are stored in our basement, are beginning to go a little soft, which means it's time to pull out all the recipes I have collected over the years dealing with potatoes. ("So once again you're left with the classic Irish man's dilemma, do I eat the potato now or let it ferment so I can drink it later," Malonly Archer)

So this morning I have decided to drop everything else I was doing, like a hot potato, and make a list of the endless possibilities those nuggets of gold can be transformed into.

I have a friend who told me the other day that her doctor informed her she was allergic to potatoes.

I don't think I could imagine anything worse. Not a day passes in my life that I don't eat potatoes in one form or another. In fact, I have an affinity with the Inca's who are reported to have prayed;

"O Creator! Thou who givest life to all things and hast made men that they may live and multiply. Multiply also the fruits of the earth, the potatoes and other food that thou hast made, that men may not suffer from hunger and misery."

It's impressive that "potatoes" are singled out while everything else is "other food." But then it's no "small potatoes" either, when we consider in our day that the International Potato Center in Peru has on hand over 5000 varieties of potatoes catalogued. (Warning!!! The puns get worse)

The history of the potato is a fascinating read. Really!!

What is amazing to me, is the attitude of the Europeans, when the conquistadores first brought the potato over from South America.

 France, who is second to none with their Parmentier recipes, once declared in the 1500's that the potato can cause narcosis, leprosy, syphilis, early death, rampant sexuality and also destroy the soil were it grows." (I'm all amazed) By the way, whenever you see a recipe with the name of Parmentier in it, you can be assured its main ingredient is the potato.

So the potato didn't get off to a good start in Europe. Even as late as the 1700's, when Fredrick the Great of Russia sent the starving peasants potatoes, they would not eat them. He had to send soldiers to "persuade them." Contrast that with the fact that in our day, the potato is the fourth largest food crop in the world proceeded by rice, wheat and maize.

In the 1800's, the potato once again made the news. Over in Ireland, where by this time, the potato had become the main source of food in the country. The potato blight hit! It has been estimated that over a million people died from starvation. The good news of that terrible tragedy is that another million Irish left Ireland during that time and came to America and Canada. So, many of us could say that we live in America because of the potato.

So, what am I going to do with this gift from the gods, which the Alaskan gold rush prospectors declared was worth its weight in gold? (Full of vitamin C, don't-cha know) It definitely means my January days of being a "couch potato" are over, but I'm ready to dive into it.

How about this!!!

Frozen Hash Browns

This is so simple you'll wonder why you ever purchased them in the store. You only have to bake whole potatoes, wrapped in aluminum foil until they are still a little firm.

Cool them down overnight. The next morning, just peel and grate them. Spread out the shreds on cookie sheets lined with wax paper and freeze.

After they freeze, gently break up the frozen hash browns and gather together into freezer bags and store in the freezer.

Some of the recipes I use hash browns in are; Hash brown soup, cheesy hash brown casserole, breakfast burritos, and of course the traditional hash browns cooked up with bacon and eggs.

Cheesy Hash Brown Casserole

2 pounds frozen hash browns
2 cans cream of mushroom soup
1 onion (chopped)
1 cup sour cream
2 cups shredded cheddar cheese
½ tsp. pepper
Bread crumbs or crushed corn flakes

Generously butter a 9 X 13 cake pan and then add the frozen hash browns.

Mix the soup, chopped onions, sour cream and shredded cheese together and pour over hash browns.

Sprinkle with pepper and enough breadcrumbs or corn flakes to cover mixture. Bake at 350 degrees for 45 minutes or until golden brown on top.

Make Ahead Burritos

15 Eggs Scrambled
1 cup chopped Peppers
2 pounds cooked Sausage
6 cups frozen hash brown potatoes
2 large onions – chopped
20 floured tortillas
Salsa
Cheese
Sour cream

In a cast iron skillet (don't go buy one, it's all I have so that's what I use) fry frozen hash browns until crispy. Set aside in a large bowl to cool. Brown the sausage with the peppers and onions, then set aside to cool in a separate bowl. Scramble eggs.

Once everything has cooled down, mix scrambled eggs, cooked sausage mixture and hash browns together.

Place ¾ cup of mixture in each floured tortilla and roll up in wax paper and then plastic wrap or aluminum foil. Place in container and freeze. Remove plastic wrap and foil before baking. Bake in the oven or microwave. Top with cheese, salsa and sour cream.

The next time you have baked potatoes for supper, throw five of six more in the oven for the gnocchi. This is also a good time to do extra potatoes for the hash browns.

How often have you thrown out that one-cup of left over mashed potatoes? That's all you need for one recipe of Fluffy Potato Doughnuts.

Fluffy Potato Doughnuts

2 cups milk
½ cup butter
1 cup sugar
1 Tablespoon salt
1 pkg. yeast
1 tsp. sugar
¼ cup lukewarm water
1 tsp. baking powder
½ tsp. baking soda
1 cup **mashed potatoes**
3 egg yolks
8 cups sifted flour
Cooking oil or lard

Scald milk. Stir in butter, 1 cup of sugar and salt. Cool to lukewarm. Sprinkle yeast and 1 teaspoon of sugar in lukewarm water, stir to dissolve and let rise.

Add risen yeast, baking powder, baking soda, mashed potatoes, egg yolks and 2 cups of flour to mixture. Beat with mixer at medium speed until smooth, about two minutes, scraping bowl occasionally.

If you have never used a mixer before, please turn off the mixer before you scrape the bowl. Just saying! If you do not have a mixer, mix with a spoon until the batter is smooth.

Gradually add remaining flour, blending well (dough will be soft) Place in lightly greased bowl; turn dough over to grease top. Cover and let rise in warm place until doubled, about two hours.

Roll out dough ¼ inch thick on floured surface. Cut with floured doughnut cutter. Place on floured waxed paper.

Cover and let rise until doubled, about 1 hour. Fry a few doughnuts at a time in hot cooking oil until each side is golden brown. Only turn once. The doughnuts should not be touching each other.

Drain on paper towels and place on a cooling rack. Spread or drizzle glaze over warm donuts with Vanilla Glaze. This recipe should make around 3 ½ dozen.

Vanilla Glaze

Combine a 1 pound box of powdered sugar, ¼ cups softened butter, 4 Tablespoons of light cream or milk and ½ tsp. of vanilla.

Beat until smooth. The amount of cream you add depends on whether or not you want to spread the glaze or drizzle the glaze over the doughnuts.

Old Fashioned Lefse

4 cups mashed or riced white potatoes
⅓ cup butter
1 Tablespoon sugar
1 ¼ cup milk
1 ¼ tsp. salt
1 ¼ to 1 ½ cups flour

Mix first five ingredients. Refrigerate until thoroughly cool. Add flour gradually and knead smooth. Depending on the size of your pan or lefse grill, take a small handful (about ⅓ cup) and roll paper-thin on a floured surface. Bake on hot griddle until golden spots form.

Turn and bake on second side. Place flat on clean towel and cover with another towel. Place several sheets of lefse on top of each other.

When cool, cut into quarters and place in plastic bags to preserve freshness. Note: Be sure dough remains cold until you are ready to roll it out.

Makes 15 large lefse.

One of the best ways in the world to use up potatoes is Klub. Find a sweet Old Norwegian grandma and steal her away for a day. Promise her anything you need to, so that she will share her secrets on making Klub. If you can't find one, not to worry, I'm happy to share my Grandmother's recipe. The Norwegian grandmothers really do have the magic touch that needs to be passed on down to posterity, or all is lost.

Klub

6 large raw potatoes grated
Flour
1 cup chopped Ham
½ cup chopped onions

Wash and peel your potatoes.

Finely grate the potatoes.

In a mixer with a bread hook attachment, mix grated raw potatoes and enough flour so that you are able to form a ball. (About baseball size) It should be a little sticky.

In a large pan, sprinkle about ½ cup of flour. The flour is to roll the potato ball around in if it becomes too sticky. Form an indentation in the ball and place a pinch of ham and onion. Close the hole and roll in flour so that you can handle it well. This should make six to eight potato balls.

Drop each ball into boiling water. Work with each potato ball for the first few minutes so they do not stick to the bottom of the pan. Slow boil for 45 minutes. Remove potato balls from water and place on a platter to cool down. Wrap in plastic wrap or zip-lock bags and freeze.

Be sure to save some out to eat for breakfast the next day. Slice very thin.

Fry the slices in butter. They are great served with fried eggs.

Enjoy!

General Douglas MacArthur summed up the importance of potatoes when he wrote the following entry in his journal. "Found a little patched-up Inn in the village of Bulson, France. Proprietor had nothing but potatoes; but what a feast he laid before me. Served them in five different courses- potato soup, potato fricassee, potatoes creamed, potato salad, and finished with potato pie. It may be because I had not eaten for 36 hours, but that meal seems about the best I ever had."

Lesson Nine ~ Beans
Don't Like Beans? Get Over It!

Just as a reminder, on the back cover of this book I wrote,

"What I am about to share with you is about survival, pure and simple.

I'll share with you principles, which if you apply any one of them, your skyrocketing grocery bill will go down noticeably. If you incorporate two or more, your bill will go down substantially. I hope you will make it your goal, after all is said and done, to cut your grocery bill in half. I assure you, it is possible." (I must say it's quite exhilarating to quote one's self!)

So you had to know that I would eventually bring up beans because most "human beans" don't know beans about beans.

It's really sad that most of us seem to equate beans as a "poor man's food." Or, that having a meal of beans and rice is a short-term fix to get out of debt, until you can get back to eating the way you did before you got yourself in debt.

I would share some of the history of the bean, but all the research I did left me scratching my head like a Neanderthal, and didn't amount to a hill of beans. "This" bean has been around for 20,000 years and "that" bean migrated from the America's 10,000 year ago, etc. One thing that everyone agrees on, is that the bean has been around since the beginning, and is not a fruit, nor is it musical.

So if I'm going to share a story about the bean, it will have to be Daniel's. You heard it in your childhood.

Daniel and his three friends were among Jewish captives taken to Babylon to serve in the king's court. They were commanded to eat the rich foods that the king served them, so that it would supposedly keep them robust.

But Daniel and his friends refused the kings food, which sent their guardian (Melzar) into a tizzy. His job was on the line if these young men didn't look well cared for.

Daniel challenged Melzar to let them eat "pulse" for ten days and drink only water. (Pulse: edible seeds of certain leguminous plants, as peas, beans, lentils etc.)

Well, the challenge was accepted and after 10 days the young men looked healthier and fairer than all the other captives. The side note is that we are told that these four young men grew in knowledge and skill, in all learning and wisdom.

Now I am not saying if we all start eating pulse that we will become Einstein's. What I will say though is that there are great benefits in eating beans.

Let's run through some of the bean bennies!

Those of you on the anti-oxidant bandwagon will appreciate that beans are high in anti-oxidants. They are high in protein, which makes them an excellent meat substitute for vegetarians. For gardeners who wish to grow their own beans, they are a well-known nitrogen fixer. (Good for the soil)

Trying to build up your food storage? Dry beans store for years when stored properly. Cholesterol watchers – beans are extremely low in cholesterol.

Beans are also a source of potassium, some amounts of iron, calcium, vitamin B, fiber and are said to be a deterrent against cancer.

Need more coaxing?

Open any cookbook in our day and usually there will be a section dealing with beans in all their variety.

For example, hummus is very popular and very easy to make, or instead of buying bean dip, make your own. I make a large amount at one time, and store it in the freezer.

If you are hungry for fresh greens during the winter, try sprouting alfalfa seeds, mung beans or chickpeas. Sprouts are also an excellent additive to salads, or used on sandwiches, instead of lettuce.

Would you believe beans are good in brownies, pies, pinto bean fudge, and cookies? While adding protein and fiber, you are cutting back on cholesterol, calories and fat. No one will ever know that beans are in the recipe.

Make a huge pot of white bean chili, minestrone soup, fejoada, Boston baked beans, or ham & bean soup and eat what you want for a few days, and put up the rest in the freezer.

Beans can also be ground into flour, curdled into tofu, tempi and miso. The list goes on.

As previously stated, beans will store for years if stored properly. If you have beans that have been in your storage for years and you feel they are too old, don't throw them out. Beans continue to lose some moisture as they age, so always remember to rotate. There are several recipes you can use them in.

The following recipe will help you to use up the beans that have been in your storage for some time.

* * * * *

Instant Refried Bean Mix

3 cups dried beans, any variety
1 tsp. ground cumin
1 tsp. chili powder
1 tsp. salt
1 Tablespoon dried minced onion
½ tsp. cayenne pepper
¼ tsp pepper

In a blender or food mill, grind beans until they resemble flour. Mix all ingredients together in a medium bowl until they are well blended. Store mix in a large airtight container or jar in a cool, dry place.

Refried Beans

¾ cup of Instant Refried Bean Mix
2 ½ cups water

Combine bean mix and water in a medium-sized saucepan. Mix with a wire whisk until combined. Bring mixture to a boil, stirring frequently, cover pan, reduce heat to low and simmer for 4-5 minutes or until thickened. Mixture will thicken more as it cools.

Years ago I was visiting Scotland where I ate something for breakfast that had never entered my mind. No, it wasn't haggis! When I asked the waitress why she served baked beans with my eggs and haggis, she simple said, "To spread on your toast, of course!" I tried it. Loved it! So I can now say, "Bean there, done that."

Lesson Ten ~ Breads

"Give Us This Day Our Daily Bread"

Bread is too serious of a topic to joke around about. Many of our fellow travelers on this planet have lost or given their lives, for a small morsel of bread.

You may be too young to remember the bread and soup lines of the great depression. Hopefully you have studied about the bread riots of 1789 in France.

According to Sylvia Neely's, A Concise History of the French Revolution, the average 18th-century worker spent half his daily wage on bread, but when the grain crops failed two years in a row, in 1788 and 1789, the price of bread shot up to 88 percent of his wages. It is a fact that in each era there will be shortages caused by drought, famine, disasters and strife.

Recently we all watched as the East Coast was hit by yet another winter storm. Like you, I shook my head as all the stores were emptied of bread and milk.

And those who arrived too late were out of luck. Yet in the Midwest we all knew about the storm a week before it hit. Didn't they get the same news report?

The other day I watched the news with sadness, as long lines of Ukrainians walked through the snow and mud, carrying everything they could carry, on their shoulders.

One of the refugees said, "There is no light, water, or communications in our town. The shops are running out of everything. Bread is brought in once a week, and it's immediately gone. Prices have risen. A plain loaf of bread cost 5.5 hryvnya (£0.23; $0.34) earlier and now its 7.5". Natalia said, "Debaltseve ran out of bread for several days."

Ukraine is not the only country in the world at this time, where teeming masses are suffering because of drought, famine and strife.

Yes, in all ages, bread is the very staff of life. If bread is all we have, it will be sufficient to get us through the vicissitudes that will inevitably come our way. Notice I said, "Will come."

I am very confident in making that statement, because history "always" repeats itself.

As terrible as I feel when I see what is happening all over our planet, I cannot travel all over the world handing out bread to the needy. We all have been placed on this earth to bloom where we are planted.

Therefore, I have one goal in mind at this time, and that is to encourage you to get started in your own family in preparing for life's changes.

One of the most important things you can do for yourself, and your family this year, is to help your family become more self-reliant, by learning to make bread.

Trust me, it's not difficult. We don't have to dig in the sand, hunt for a few twigs to make fire, place the bread on top of the coals, and then bury it all with more sand until our bread is baked. Oh yes, and be sure you brush all the sand off before serving.

I have to tell you, when I first started making bread, any brick layer would have been happy to use my loaves of bread for any building project.

Don't be discouraged!

Think of the types of bread your family enjoys eating, and begin there. If you have little children, there is no more enjoyable activity to engage them in. They will play with dough for hours if you let them.

When my husband retired, he decided he wanted to be the bread maker in the family. He has been working on this project for ten years, and I have to say the bread he makes is better than any that I ever made.

He makes 8 loaves every two weeks. Now you would think 8 loaves would last us longer than two weeks. In normal circumstances it would, but he gets a great deal of satisfaction in handing it out to the neighbors. So in reality, we usually end up with two loaves for ourselves.

Jose Marti, who died at the age of 42 fighting for Cuban independence from Spain, said it well: "If I survive, I will spend my whole life at the oven door, seeing that no one is denied bread, and so as to give a lesson of charity, especially to those who did not bring flour."

So where do we start? With the ingredients of course!

The wonderful thing about making your own bread, is that all the ingredients store for great lengths of time.

All you need in your pantry for the simple breads are, yeast, salt, oil, sugar/honey, whole wheat or white flour.

When I say simple breads, I am referring to breads like; pizza dough, tortillas, English muffins, bagels, pita, and Indian fry bread.

Other breads like pretzels and French bread might call for sesame or poppy seeds to be sprinkled on the crust. That of course is optional.

The whole wheat bread we make does not call for eggs, but breads like sweet dinner rolls do.

If your favorite bread is lefse, then you will also need to have potatoes on hand. Although for many years now, I know purist Norwegians who are using potato flakes and swear by them. The benefit of potato flakes is that they store well in your pantry!

Bread has a multitude of wonderful attributes that make it worthwhile investing your time and effort.

Besides the fact that pounding and kneading the dough is therapeutic, baking it makes your home smell like heaven on earth.

But the most important reason for learning the skill of bread making is that it can fill your family's tummies when times get tough.

James Beard said; "Good bread is the most fundamentally satisfying of all foods; and good bread with fresh butter, the greatest of feasts."

And I will add my two cents worth by adding that on a cold winter's night a feast can also be a cup of hot chocolate with toasted homemade bread liberally spread with butter.

Here are a few of our favorite bread recipes;

* * * * *

Oatmeal Molasses Bread

6 cups hot water
3 cups old fashioned oats
⅔ cup honey
¾ cup oil
2 Tablespoons salt
½ cup sunflower seeds
½ pumpkin seeds
½ cup molasses
3 cups whole-wheat flour
3 pkgs. (3 tsp.) yeast
Approximately 9 cups of white flour

In ½ cup of warm water, add the yeast and sprinkle ½ tsp of sugar on top. Set aside.

Mix first 8 ingredients (water, oats, honey, oil, salt, seeds, molasses, whole-wheat flour) and mix well. Make sure mixture has cooled off somewhat, then add the yeast.

Stir again and gradually begin adding the rest of the flour. I alternate between one cup of whole-wheat flour and one cup of white until l have used all the whole-wheat and then continue on with the white. When you can no longer stir with a spoon, continue to add flour one cup at a time and mix with your hands.

When the dough becomes very dense, begin adding flour at about 1/4 cup at a time. You will know when the dough is ready, as it will no longer stick to your hands or the side of the bowl. It will also be elastic.

Form into a ball and cover with a towel and let raise to double in size. Punch down and form loaves. Let rise to double in size. This should make 6 to 8 loaves.

Bake at 350° for approximately 35 to 45 minutes.

90-Minute Soft Pretzels

1 cup warm water
1 pkg. dry yeast (1 tsp.)
1 Tablespoon sugar
1 tsp. salt
1 Tablespoon butter
3 ¼ to 3 ¾ cups all-purpose flour

Coating

1 egg yolk (save white of egg for the French Bread mentioned below)
1 Tablespoon water
Coarse salt
Poppy seeds or sesame seeds for toppings

Combine in order and knead until elastic. Let rise until double in a greased bowl. Divide into quarters, then thirds.

Form into pretzels. Beat egg yolk and water together and brush on pretzels. Sprinkle your favorite topping on pretzel and let rise until double.

Bake 15 minutes at 375°

Makes one dozen pretzels.

French Bread

7-8 cups of un-sifted flour
1 tsp. sugar
1 Tablespoon salt
3 pkgs. yeast
3 Tablespoons softened butter
2 ½ cups very warm water
Corn meal
1 egg while (beaten)
1 Tablespoon of cold water
Sesame seeds or poppy seeds

In a large bowl, mix 2 ½ cups flour, sugar, salt and dry yeast. Add butter. Gradually add water to dry ingredients and beat two minutes at medium speed with electric mixer.

Gradually add remaining flour. Divide into three or four pieces, shaping like a jellyroll. Grease pans and sprinkle with corn meal. Combine egg white and water and brush on bread.

Sprinkle with sesame or poppy seeds. Let rise in a warm place for at least an hour. It depends on how warm your house is. They should be over double in size.

Bake at 450° for 20 to 25 minutes.

Pizza Dough

2 pkgs. dry yeast
3 cups warm water
1 Tablespoon sugar
1 tsp. salt
7 ½ cups flour

Sprinkle yeast over lukewarm water. Add pinch of sugar to yeast to make it work faster if desired. Let yeast work to a bubble.

Add sugar and salt. Add two cups of flour and beat with mixer for 2 minutes. Stir in enough remaining flour to make the dough soft. It needs to be pliable and not overly sticky. Let dough rest for an hour at the least. Grease pizza pans and sprinkle corn meal on pans. Form pizza crusts on table and then place on pans.

Makes approximately four medium crusts.

Dinner Rolls

2 cups evaporated milk
½ cup sugar
2 tsp. salt
½ cup butter
2 pkgs. Yeast
½ cup warm water
2 eggs (beaten)
7 to 7 ½ cups flour

Heat milk, sugar and salt in a saucepan on stove until sugar and salt are dissolved. Do not boil. Remove from stove and pour into mixing bowl. Drop in 1 stick or ½ cup frozen butter. I use frozen butter because it will cool down the milk faster.

Meanwhile have 2 packages of yeast dissolving in ½ cup of warm water.

When Milk mixture has cooled down sufficiently, add the yeast mixture. In a mixer, stir in 2 beaten eggs. Gradually add from 7 to 7 ½ cups of flour.

Knead until the dough mixture no longer sticks to the side of the bowl. Let rise double. Punch down and form into rolls and let rise again. Bake at 400° degrees for about 20 to 25 minutes. With this recipe you can also make sticky buns.

English Muffins

1 pkg. dry Yeast
1 cup warm Water
2 teaspoons Salt
1 tsp. sugar
¼ cup lard
3 cups flour
2 Tablespoons cornmeal

Dissolve yeast in water in a large mixing bowl. Add salt, sugar, lard and flour. Stir until smooth.

Roll dough ¼ inch thick on floured surface. Cut into 3 ½ inch circles.

Sprinkle ungreased baking sheet with1 tablespoon cornmeal and place circles on a baking sheet.

Sprinkle remaining 1 Tablespoon over circles.

Cover, let rise in a warm place until light to the touch, about one hour. Heat an ungreased electric griddle or skillet to 375°.

Transfer circles to griddle. Cook 7 minutes on each side and cool. Split, toast and serve with butter and your favorite jam.

Makes 10 to 12 muffins.

Baking Powder Biscuits

5 cups sifted flour
2 cups cake flour
3 Tablespoons baking powder
1½ tsp. baking soda
¾ cup of lard
3 cups buttermilk
3 Tablespoons melted butter

Set your oven at 450°. This recipe will make approximately 30 biscuits. Freeze excess biscuits for future use.

Sift the first four ingredients together into a large bowl and blend in lard with your hands to a pea size consistency.

In the center, dig out a well and pour in the buttermilk. Gently stir with a fork until almost blended.

Place mixture on floured counter top and knead a few times, just enough until the dough comes together.
Form into a large rectangle and fold into thirds as if you are folding a letter.

Once again, pat it down into a large rectangle and fold into thirds.

After the second time, use your rolling pin and roll out into a 12 x 18 inch rectangle about ½ inch thick.

I use my pizza cutter to cut 2½ x 1¾ inch rectangles.

Cut a piece of parchment paper to fit a large cookie sheet and brush with melted butter.

Line your biscuits up on the cookie sheet ⅛ inch apart and brush with melted butter. Bake for 15 minutes or until golden brown.

Pie Crust

4 cups flour
1 tsp. salt
1 Tablespoon sugar
1 ½ cup lard
1 tsp. baking powder
½ cup very cold water
1 egg beaten
1 Tablespoon vinegar

Place the ½ cup of cold water in the freezer before you mix the dry ingredients. In a separate bowl mix the flour, salt, sugar, lard and baking powder. These four ingredients need to reach the consistency of cornmeal. Remove the water from the freezer and stir in the vinegar and beaten egg. Slowly add these three ingredients to the flour mixture. Mix and handle as little as possible   Roll out between two pieces of floured wax paper. This allows you to transfer the piecrust to the pan with greater ease.

Makes 3 double crust or six single crust pies.

Indian Fry Bread

2 cups flour
⅛ cup dry milk
2 tsp. baking powder (heaping)
1 Tablespoon sugar
1 Tablespoon vegetable oil
1 cup hot water

Mix dry ingredients. In a separate measuring cup add oil & hot water. Slowly pour water mixture to flour mixture until dough forms. Set for 10 minutes. Tear into golf ball size portions and roll out each ball as you go. Fry until golden brown on each side. Serve as taco shells or eat with butter and honey.

Sourdough Recipes

Starter:

2 cups flour
2 cups thick potato water
2 Tablespoons sugar

Boil some potatoes with jackets on until they fall to pieces. Remove skins from pot and mash potatoes making a puree. Cool.

Add more water to make sufficient liquid, if necessary. The richer the potato water, the richer the Starter. Place all ingredients in a pot.

Beat until a smooth creamy batter. Cover. Set aside in a warm place to start fermentation. This makes what is called the "sponge". The process takes about 3 days.

Sourdough Pancakes or Waffles

When ready to make pancakes or any other recipe, take out ½ cup of sponge and place in refrigerator in loosely covered crock or jar.

This is your Starter for everything you make into sourdough.

2 tsp. soda or 1 tsp. soda & 1 tsp. of baking powder
2 eggs
2 Tablespoons sugar
3 Tablespoons oil

Mix and fry on buttered skillet.

Sourdough French Bread

Set Sponge for French bread by removing Starter from refrigerator the night before and add 1 cup of Flour and 1 cup of Water to Starter. Let work overnight. Then remove 1 cup Starter for the following recipe. Return remaining ½ cup Starter to refrigerator.

Plan on 24 hours from start to finish for this sourdough recipe.

1½ cup warm water
1 cup starter
4 cups un-sifted flour
2 tsp. sugar
2 tsp. salt

Combine ingredients and mix well. Place in crock and leave at room temperature about 18 hours or until sponge has doubled in size. Stir in 1 cup flour that has been mixed with ½ tsp. soda: the resulting dough will be very stiff.

Turn dough out onto a floured board and knead, adding 1 cup of flour as needed. Knead until smooth – at least 8 minutes, until the dough cannot absorb any more flour.

Shape into 2 oblong rolls or one large round loaf. Place on a lightly greased cookie sheet, cover and place in a warm place for 3 to 4 hours, or until nearly doubled in size.

Just before baking, brush with water; make diagonal slashes in the top with a sharp knife. Place a shallow pan of hot water in the oven. Bake in a 400° oven until crust is a medium dark brown (about 45 minutes for oblong loaves – 50 minutes for the large round loaf)

For a heavier and tougher crust, remove loaf from oven 10 minutes before it is done; brush with salted water and return to very hot oven (425°) for the remaining time.

For a more tender crust, do not place pan of water in over and brush unbaked loaf with salad oil or butter instead or water.

Sourdough tips:

- ❖ In pancakes and waffles, add soda just before baking.

- ❖ Always use a wooden spoon to stir batter. Do not mix in the sourdough pot.

- ❖ You should refrigerate your starter unless you plan to use it every two days.
- ❖ Never place starter in metal containers. Use glass or crock ware.

- ❖ Add flour and water the night before to build up the quantity of starter needed – (Approximately equal amounts of flour and water.) This will allow the Sourdough enzymes to work 10 hours and remove most of the starch, leaving a protein food.

- ❖ Sugar is used as a booster to make the enzymes work faster. It is not used to sweeten the Sourdough.

- ❖ Sugar is used to brown. Too much sugar will make the Sourdough rubbery.

- ❖ Soda is used to sweeten – it reacts against the acid in the Sourdough.

- ❖ Lightly cover the Sourdough Pot. Never seal with a tight lid as Sourdough needs to breath. A piece of cheese cloth is an excellent cover for the Sourdough Pot.

- ❖ Sourdough may be kept in the refrigerator when not in constant use. It becomes dormant. Remember to take it out at least a day before using to get the Sourdough enzymes working again. Add flour and water. Keep warm.

Lesson 11 ~ Mixes

I believe it was in the 70's when I first became interested in making my own mixes. I discovered that anything that could be purchased in the grocery store, was first made in someone's home.

Over the years, I have also become alarmed at the increased use of MSG and High Fructose Corn Syrup, added to just about everything I purchase in the store. I think the biggest surprise was the day I was going to buy a can of cranberry sauce, and was shocked that the first ingredient was HFCS. That's when I decided to put up my own cranberry sauce.

I'm not going to get into the debate of whether or not these added ingredients are harmful to your health or not. Personally, when it comes to my own health, I don't want to take the chance.

Since I was a teenager during the sixties, you would probably think that my favorite breakfast cereal was Sugar Puffs. Everyone had a box of Sugar Puffs in their cupboard. But, not so! My favorite was Grape Nuts.

I was in hog heaven when I discovered a recipe for making homemade grape nuts. I was pleasantly surprised at how easy they were to make.

Homemade Grape Nuts

3 cups whole-wheat flour
¾ cup sour milk or buttermilk
2 Tablespoons baking soda
½ tsp. salt
1 cup brown sugar

Mix all dry ingredients together on a large cookie sheet. Pour sour milk overall and mix with your hands until very fine. Place in a pre-heated oven at 350° and bake for fifteen minutes or until golden brown. Remove from oven and crumble with your hands.

You can let it cool down a little, but not too much, because it is more difficult to crumple when cooled. Return mixture to oven for at least five more minutes, or until grape nuts are thoroughly hardened. Store in a gallon glass container.

My husband's favorite mix is the whole-wheat pancake mix, which he also uses in his awesome waffles.

Whole Wheat Pancake/Waffle Mix

¾ cup baking powder
3 Tablespoons salt
2 Tablespoons cream of tarter
2½ cups non-instant dry milk
½ cup sugar
10 cups whole-wheat flour
10 cups white flour
2 pounds (4 cups) lard

Sift all dry ingredients together in a large bowl. Cut the lard into the dry mixture until it is the consistency of cornmeal using your hands, a fork or pastry utensil.

This can be stored in a gallon jar. We have an extra fridge in our garage that we use for large items like this. Another way to store the mix is to divide it into 3-cup portions and pour into zip-lock bags. We use 3-cup portions because that is what is used in each pancake recipe.

Here is all you have to do to make pancakes: To 3 cups of the mix, add one egg and 1 ½ cup of water. Stir and let sit for five minutes. This makes around 15 four-inch pancakes.

Making waffles is just as easy although there is an extra step. To the 3-cup mix add 3 egg yolks and 2¼ cups of water. Beat the 3 egg whites until they form white peaks. Fold the whipped egg whites into the waffle mixture.

Pour ½ cup onto your hot waffle iron and cook until crispy. This will make about 16 four-inch waffles. Remember, if you make too many waffles you can freeze them for later use. Pop them in the toaster on those mornings when everyone is in a hurry.

* * * * *

There are mixes for cakes, brownies, muffins, tortillas (see the previous lesson on breads) cookies, puddings and seasonings.

The cookie mixes are some of my favorites because of the time it saves and they taste better than store bought.

Think of the times your child informed you as you were helping them with their homework in the evening. "Oh, Mom, by the way, it's my turn to bring cookies tomorrow."

"No problem, you say, just get the slice and bake cookie rolls we made up a few weeks ago, from the freezer and getter done." It will be part of their homework.

It will be no stress on anyone's part, because, you thought ahead by taking a few hours on a Saturday morning, and mixed up peanut butter, chocolate chip, oatmeal and sugar cookie dough. You taught them how to roll each cookie dough batch into three to four logs, wrapped them in wax paper, then aluminum foil, marked them and placed them in the freezer.

Now I know you are probably thinking. "It's easier to go to the store and buy a package of cookies." I agree with you. It is easier. But "what if" for some reason you couldn't get to the store or you didn't have the money to purchase what you needed at that moment?

Besides, if someone in the family volunteers to bring something to an event, they need to take responsibility with the follow-through. By taking the rolls of dough from the freezer, slicing each cookie and placing it on a cookie sheet, they experience the process, can take pride in doing what they said, and the added bonus is tasting fresh baked cookies with a glass of milk, as they finish their homework.

Some other mixes you may want to consider are seasoning mixes like taco, chili, sloppy Joes, spaghetti and Italian dressing mix. These packets of premade mixes in the store have become quite expensive.

Most people have the basic spices on hand already in their cupboard, so making your own packets should not be a great expense. Although, I would advise everyone to take an inventory of the spices you have to see how fresh they are.

Here is an Italian Dressing mix you will love;

Italian Dressing Mix

1 tsp. dry minced onions
1 Tbs. crushed dried parsley
¼ tsp. ground oregano
½ tsp. crushed dried sweet basil
¼ tsp. ground thyme or marjoram
½ tsp. celery seed
¼ tsp. garlic powder
2 tbs. Parmesan cheese
1 ½ tsp. sugar
⅛ tsp. salt
Pinch of pepper

Combine and mix all ingredients well. Add ½ cup of your favorite vinegar (I use balsamic) and 1 cup olive oil. Mix well and let set for at least an hour, (the older it gets, the better it tastes) and use on your favorite pasta, or green salad. We love to use this dressing when we have pizza to dip the crust in. The crust no longer gets thrown away.

Make a list of the mixes you purchase, and then do a search to see if you can make that mix yourself. You will be pleasantly surprised.

Flour Tortilla Mix

10 cups of flour
2 heaping Tablespoons of baking powder
1 heaping cup of lard
2 teaspoons salt

In a large mixing bowl, use your hands to mix all ingredients together into a cornmeal consistency. Transfer to a gallon jar or zip-lock bag and store in a cool place. I keep mine in the fridge. It will store for months but I find that I use this mix so often that I really don't have to worry about whether or not it will spoil.

Flour Tortillas

2 ½ cups **Tortilla Mix**
½ cup very warm water

In a medium bowl, combine **Tortilla Mix** and water. Stir with a fork until mixture forms a ball. Turn out onto a lightly floured surface. Knead about 10 times until dough forms a soft ball. Divide into 10 balls and let the dough rest for an hour.

Preheat your griddle. On a lightly floured surface, roll out balls to 9 inch circles. If you are doing this for the first time, don't worry so much about the shape. I have made hundreds of tortillas and they still take on the shape of Texas. Making tortillas is a little like making pancakes. For some reason the first one never turns out.

Transfer the tortilla to the preheated un-greased cast iron skillet. It usually takes cooking the first one to adjust the heat about 15 seconds on one side or until bubbles form. Turn tortilla; cook 15 seconds longer. Remove from pan. Place on a cloth towel with the other half of the towel to keep warm.

Makes 10 tortillas.

Time Saver: When you have time make up several dozen, let them cool and freeze. All you have to do is heat them up again when you are in a hurry and want to have a taco night

Lesson 12 ~ 5 Meals, 1 Chicken

In the Lesson titled "The Principle of Divide & Multiply," I mentioned that I make five meals out of one chicken.

Usually when I share this piece of information with people, their eyes grow wide and they exclaim, "Wow, they must really grow gihugic chickens where you live." Or they look at me like I'm giving them a cock and bull story.

Making 5 meals from one chicken is not just a principle for tough times. It helps with your menu planning, budgeting and "feathering your nest."

In order for anyone to apply this principle, there needs to be a paradigm shift in the way we use meat in our meal planning. I probably need to walk on egg shells here, because I know so many of you are going to tell me how much you love meat, and your family demands it for every meal.

All I'm saying is, if that's the case – take the meat you have planned for your meals and spread it over several meals.

For our discussion today we are going to focus on the "versatile" chicken.

First of all, when whole chickens go on sale, buy several. In fact, whenever any of your favorite meats go on sale, purchase more than what you need and freeze for it future use.

In this age of chicken nuggets, I would be willing to bet that most people do not know how to cut up a whole chicken anymore.

Not a problem. All you have to do is check YouTube and I'm sure there will be an abundance of "how to" videos.

Cutting up a chicken is not difficult and takes very little time. Now don't let this ruffle your feathers, but, if you are queasy about getting your hands messy, get over it!

This is survival in the kitchen 101.

I only buy whole chickens because they are less expensive and I can inspect the whole chicken and not worry about buying a package of "parts" that may have been gleaned from a chicken that is less than healthy. (Yes, they do that)

Everyone has their favorite recipes that call for chicken. Our favorites are fried chicken, biscuits and gravy, lemon linguine, tortellini soup and stir-fry. Yes – all five meals made with one chicken.

Maybe your household likes Chicken Kiev, or Chicken & Broccoli Bake. Another good chicken extender is Hawaiian Chicken. The list goes on forever what you can do with just a small amount of chicken.

It is important to remember, that the meat is not the focus of the dinner. So let's look at our first of the five meals that are calculated for a family of three.

1. **Fried Chicken** (thigh, ½ of a breast, 2 legs, wing)

Think about the side dishes that will round out this meal, which depends on what your family likes. When I think of a fried chicken dinner, I like to have potato or pasta salad, a vegetable and dinner rolls.

Twice baked potatoes, French fries or mashed potatoes are also a good call.

If you choose mashed potatoes with gravy, be sure to make more gravy than you need for the one meal. The leftover gravy will be added to the next meal below.

If you are not making gravy with your fried chicken, be sure to save the pan you fried the chicken in. Pour off most, but not all of the grease that remains in the pan after frying.

Let the pan cool, cover and place in the fridge until morning.

2. **Biscuits and gravy.** (Drippings from frying the chicken)

This is my husband's favorite breakfast. Every time I prepare this meal he will sit down at the table and exclaim; "Now I know you love me!"

I make gravy from the drippings I saved in the pan from the night before. If I boiled potatoes the night before, I always save the potato water to add to the gravy as it makes the gravy thicker.

The biscuits can be made ahead of time if you don't want to feel like your "running around like a chicken with its head cut off," in the morning, but they are much tastier if made fresh.

Seriously, biscuits are very easy and quick to make.

3. **Lemon Chicken Linguine** (one breast)

This is my personal favorite and all you need is one chicken breast.
I usually serve this with a green salad and garlic or cheese bread. Believe me, this is a filling meal and scrumptious.

4. **Ravioli, Tortellini or Macaroni Soup** (back, neck, wing)

There are probably a hundred different soups you can make with chicken parts but this one happens to be one of our favorites. Some others are Greek lime chicken soup, Ravioli and chicken and dumplings.

Making chicken soup also helps me use up the vegetables I have saved in the freezer.

5. Stir Fry (thigh, ½ breast)

Keeping with the principle that meat should be used as a flavoring for your recipes, only a cup of chopped chicken is used in the stir fry recipe I use.

After adding all the rice, and a multitude of vegetables to the chicken, you have enough stir fry to last more than one meal. And it makes a great meal to take to work the next day.

With these five meals you have used everything on the chicken but the feet and feathers. Remember that this same principle can be used with beef, or pork roast, ham, turkey or any other meat you have on hand, or purchased on sale.

* * * * *

Five Meals – One Chicken Recipes

Fried Chicken Dinner

Thigh, ½ breast, 2 legs, 1 wing of chicken
Cast iron skillet
Oil or lard
Brown paper bag

I like to cut up my own chicken so that I can make several meals out of it.

Since there are only two of us at home now and because we have learned how to take the focus off meat as being the main part of the meal we only use a wing, 2 legs, one thigh and half a breast for frying. But we always have left over chicken.

I use lard that we have rendered in the spring to fry the chicken.

Many people, especially in the South, will soak the cut up chicken in buttermilk for an hour before frying, because it makes more crunchies on the chicken. Most of the time, I don't have buttermilk on hand, so I consider it optional.

In a brown paper bag, I add the following ingredients.

1 cup flour
¼ cup corn meal
½ cup potato flakes
Salt and pepper to taste

Add cut-up chicken to the flour mixture in the bag. Twist the top of the bag shut and shake vigorously.

Make sure your oil or melted lard is hot before you add the coated chicken to the frying pan.

Brown each piece on both sides to seal in the juices. You will then want to turn down the heat and continue to simmer, (about twenty minutes depending on how thick the chicken piece is}. The thigh and the leg always take longer.

When each piece is done, remove from the pan and place on a platter lined with a paper towel to absorb extra grease.

When you add mashed potatoes, a vegetable or salad and beans to this, you have more than enough for a sumptuous meal.

Biscuits served with Chicken Gravy

Save the drippings in the pan from the fried chicken. As soon as the pan cools, cover it and store in fridge. In the morning remove pan from fridge and pour two cups of water in the pan, along with 1 chicken bouillon and bring to a boil. To one cup of water, add 3 Tablespoons of cornstarch or flour. Make sure there are no lumps. Slowly add to boiling water while using a whisk. Bring to a boil and stir for several minutes. If too thick, add more water. Pour over homemade biscuits and serve with eggs and juice.

Lemon Chicken Linguine

1 large Chicken Breast cut up
3 Tablespoons Butter
2 Tablespoons Chives
1 lemon
Salt and pepper
1 pint of sour cream
1 clove garlic
1 pound linguine

Sauté cut up chicken breast in butter. Add chives and chopped garlic. Continue to sauté. Grate Lemon and add grated pieces to chicken. Squeeze remaining lemon into mixture. When chicken in fully cooked, add the sour cream. If too thick, add more lemon. Pour mixture over cooked linguine just before serving.

Serve with Parmesan Cheese French Bread, and a Salad.

Parmesan Cheese French Bread

Mix equal amounts of butter, mayonnaise and Parmesan cheese together. Spread mixture onto sliced French bread. Place in an oven pre-heated to 425° and cook until cheese mixture is golden brown.

Ravioli, Tortellini or Macaroni Soup

Chicken Parts (back, neck and wing)
6 cups Water
1 large Can Tomatoes
2 small cans Tomato Sauce
1 ½ cups chopped onion
½ cup each of corn, celery, green beans or other vegetables
¼ cup parsley
2 garlic cloves, minced
¾ tsp. dried basil
½ tsp. dried oregano
½ tsp. salt
½ tsp. sugar
¼ tsp. pepper
¼ tsp. thyme
1 chicken bouillon
¼ cup parmesan
1 pkg. pasta of choice

Slow boil chicken parts for 30 minutes or until meat falls off bones. Remove chicken from water and remove all meat. Return chicken meat to water. Add all remaining ingredients except the Parmesan cheese and Pasta. Slow boil for 30 minutes.
If you want the soup ready in a shorter time, cook the pasta ahead of time. Add the cooked pasta to the soup five minutes before you serve. If you throw in uncooked pasta the preparation time is longer. Have fresh grated Parmesan cheese on the table to sprinkle onto the soup. Serve with soft cooked pretzels, baguette, bread sticks or crackers.

This will probably make more soup than your family can eat in one setting. When cooled, pour into containers and freeze for a later meal.

Stir Fry with Chicken

4 cups uncooked Rice
1 cup uncooked Chicken
3 tablespoons Oil
1 large Onion chopped
3 cloves Garlic chopped
1 piece Ginger
1 cup celery
1 cup chopped carrots
1 cup peas
1 cup corn
1 cup green beans
1 can water chestnuts (chopped)
1 cup green or various colored peppers
soy sauce

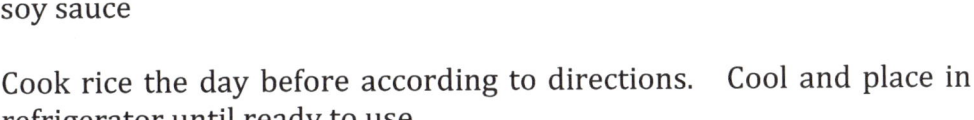

Cook rice the day before according to directions. Cool and place in refrigerator until ready to use.

Heat a large skillet or wok and pour in oil. Place chopped chicken, onion, garlic and ginger in heated skillet and stir until chicken is cooked. Add all the vegetables and water chestnuts and cook until vegetables are cooked, but crunchy. You don't want vegetables to be overly cooked.

Lastly, add the cold rice and mix everything together. Sprinkle with soy sauce. Remove the ginger unless someone in your family likes it. Serve with a green salad sprinkled with rice vinegar.

~That's All She Wrote ~

After sharing these lessons on principles that will help you cut your food budget in half, my brain is empty. That's all she wrote!

Back in October of 2014, I decided I would try an experiment by putting my own advice to work.

From the 1st of October to March 1st I decided I would try as much as possible to live off the food we had put up during the fall.

With the gleaning, canning, drying and freezing I was sure we would have to make very few trips to the grocery store.

So I took an inventory of all that we had put up. I made up menu's for a month at a time and put my shoulder to the wheel.

During the middle of March, I assessed my experiment. I'm not too pleased with the end result. During the six months from the beginning of October to the end of of March, I spent $350 dollars on groceries. It would have been half that amount, had I not sent my husband to the store.

I knew we would need things like butter, eggs and various fresh items to supplement what was already in our food storage, and even though I sent him with a list, it just didn't work.

He would walk in the door upon returning from town with a big grin on his face and say, "Boy, wait till you see what I bought, it was on sale."

Even though we had sat down and agreed on the experiment together, he was so used to buying the item that was the weekly leader/loss that he kept forgetting that we were on a different page for the winter.

So "If" we had adhered to the plan we probably would have spent around $250 during the five months. As I have shared this little experiment with others, I have been assured by almost all, that they think $350 is amazing for five months.

As I navigated these five months, I followed the principles that were shared in these lessons.

Another canning, freezing and dehydrating season is now over, and I am confident that I can embark on my little experiment again. We have been abundantly blessed.

So beginning in October, I will sit down with my hubby, and we will go over the plan again, and see if we can live off what we have put up with as little trips to the grocery store as possible.

I hope you have gleaned from these lessons and principles, when applied, will bring your family greater security and peace.

Thank you for
"Putting Up With Leona"

Notes

Notes

46338069R00072

Made in the USA
Lexington, KY
30 October 2015